Swinging
from My Heels

ALSO BY ALAN SHIPNUCK

Bud, Sweat, & Tees

The Battle for Augusta National

Swinging from My Heels

Confessions of an LPGA Star

Christina Kim
and Alan Shipnuck

BLOOMSBURY

New York   Berlin   London

Published by Bloomsbury USA, New York

All papers used by Bloomsbury USA are natural, recyclable products made from wood grown in well-managed forests. The manufacturing processes conform to the environmental regulations of the country of origin.

LIBRARY OF CONGRESS CATALOGING-IN-PUBLICATION DATA

Kim, Christina.
Swinging from my heels : confessions of an LPGA star / Christina Kim and Alan Shipnuck.
p. cm.
ISBN 978-1-60819-088-1
1. Kim, Christina.   2. Golfers—United States—Biography.   3. Women golfers—United States—Biography.   I. Shipnuck, Alan, 1973–   II. Title.
GV964.K495A3 2010
796.352092—dc22
[B]
2010001310

First U.S. Edition 2010

1 3 5 7 9 10 8 6 4 2

Typeset by Westchester Book Group
Printed in the United States of America by Worldcolor Fairfield

To my family, for teaching me all of life's lessons and believing in me when everyone else thought I was crazy.—CK

For all the amazing ladies in my life: Abigail, Michayla, Olivia, and Frances. And for Ben, too.—AS

CONTENTS

PREFACE

This book began with a nice steak, medium rare. It was in the fall of 2008 that I got a surprise dinner invitation from Alan Shipnuck. We've been buddies going back to 2004, when he wrote a colorful feature about me for *Sports Illustrated*. Alan is also the author of my all-time favorite golf book, *Bud, Sweat, & Tees*, the racy Rich Beem story that was a million miles from all of the boring PGA Tour tales that had preceded it. During our meal, Alan pitched the idea of collaborating on a book about the LPGA in which I could serve as a tour guide to one of sport's most fascinating subcultures. It was such a delicious idea that we were sketching out the chapters long before the chocolate mousse had been polished off.

The LPGA is probably the last unexplored corner of a sports universe defined by media oversaturation. While men's golf practically has its own library, no one has ever done a serious book about life on the LPGA. The oversight is baffling given the tour's rich history and the complex issues faced by today's players.

The LPGA was founded in 1950 by thirteen pioneering women including Babe Zaharias, whom I consider the greatest athlete of the twentieth century, male or female. That first season featured fourteen tournaments with a total purse of fifty thousand dollars. The LPGA grew in fits and starts from there, held together by the passion and perseverance of the founders. It wasn't until 1963 that any event was televised nationally. By 2007 nine LPGA golfers had been named the Associated Press's female athlete of the year. In '08 the LPGA boasted thirty-four events with a total purse of $64.1 million.

In addition to enduring the exquisite torture of tournament golf, the young women on tour struggle with many issues that are all but unknown to their male counterparts, including negative body images, overzealous fathers, xenophobia, money problems, and whispers about their sexuality. All of these delicate topics and many more are discussed in this book because from the very beginning I have been committed to a raw, real, no-holds-barred look at life on tour.

I know this approach may ruffle a few feathers, but nobody loves the LPGA more than I do. I've always done everything possible to support and promote the tour, and this book is no exception. There are many wonderful things about the LPGA and its diverse membership, and I have enjoyed putting these stories on paper. At the same time, I think it's important to be honest about the many challenges we face, both as individuals and as the most high-profile women's sports organization in the world. Alan once put it another way: I'm not going to help the LPGA by producing a boring book.

This narrative is organized around the twenty-seven tournaments that constituted my 2009 season. I hope it reads less like a traditional sports tome and more like an intimate diary. It was a roller-coaster year, on and off the course. Enjoy the ride.

CHAPTER 1

Blue Hawaii

Bawling on the practice putting green, heartbroken, is not exactly how I wanted to prepare for the first tournament of the season, but sometimes life gets in the way of golf. I had just finished my Monday practice round at Turtle Bay, site of the SBS Championship, when Pat Hurst came up to me and said, "I heard about you and Mark." Pat is a matronly veteran who's always looked out for me, and as soon as I saw the concern in her eyes, I lost it. She enveloped me in a big hug, and right there on the putting green I started sobbing on her shoulder. We had a long talk about heartbreak, and Pat shared some very personal stories from her life. I was grateful for her perspective but eventually I hid my watery eyes behind a pair of sunglasses and went back to working on my putting. Then a procession of colleagues began coming up to me to say they had heard the news, beginning with Suzann Pettersen. On the golf course she's an intense competitor, but Suzann was so kind and comforting that of course more crying ensued. No sooner had she left than my close friend Morgan Pressel ran up to give me a hug, and she was followed by Stacy Prammanasudh, and on and on it went. It was like the receiving line at a wake, and I wound up standing on the green for four hours of blubbering, interrupted only by intermittent lag-putting.

Mark Britton had been my boyfriend for two and a half years, and we had broken up just a few weeks before the SBS. I had been dealing with it pretty much alone at home in Orlando and in some ways the breakup didn't feel real until I arrived at Turtle Bay and had to face all of the other players and all of Mark's fellow caddies. We had been the Brad and Angelina of the LGPA, minus the movie-star looks—the source of endless entertainment and gossip for people, and I had always enjoyed the attention. Now instead of laughs I was eliciting pity. The fuss being made over me on the practice green was just the first glimpse of how much my life had already changed.

Mark and I had met in a hotel lobby in Mexico City in March 2006 and clicked right away. He was caddying for my friend Helen Alfredsson, and over the next few months he and I would chat whenever we crossed paths. The LPGA is as insular and gossipy as high school. I began to hear whispers that Mark had a thing for me, but he was too shy to make the first move. That changed a few months after our first meeting when, following the final round of the Evian Masters, a bunch of players and caddies gathered at a pub in picturesque Évian-les-Bains, France. A few drinks helped loosen up Mark, as did my outfit—I have to say, I was looking rather saucy in itty-bitty Daisy Duke shorts and a sheer white top that pretty much served no purpose. We counted that day at the pub as our first date and quickly fell into a blissfully happy romance. Exploring the world together was a blast, but we also enjoyed many quiet nights watching a movie in the hotel or just talking about our days. Being a tour pro can be a very lonely life, and I was grateful to have Mark by my side. My previous five relationships had all expired around the six-month mark and, even in good times, those guys rarely came on the road with me. Mark was the first boyfriend whom I introduced to my old-school Korean parents, and all the ensuing drama forced me to grow up and assume more control of my life and my career. I thought we were going to be together forever, but everything began to fall apart in the fall of 2008, beginning with a big talk Mark and I had while in Japan for the Mizuno Classic.

One night in our hotel room in Japan, Mark confided to me that he was anxious to start a family. Unfortunately, our clocks were ticking differently. At the time he was thirty-five and I was only twenty-four, and at least seven years from being ready for children. I have so much left to accomplish as a golfer, and in a lot of ways I view having kids as a reward for a successful career. A few golfers, like Juli Inkster and Laura Diaz, have balanced being a mom with a lot of success on the course, but plenty of others have fallen off the radar after popping out a few little ones. Bottom line, it's fifty-fifty you'll never be the same as a player. And then there's my long bucket list. I have so much living to do—I want to skydive, get scuba certified, take up underwater photography, and so much more. Having kids is the end of being selfish, and right now I'm quite happy being self-centered and petulant. I told Mark all of this that night in Japan, and it was a pretty strained conversation.

After the tournament he flew home to Scotland, as scheduled, to be with his family and to caddie for a friend at the Ladies European Tour Qualifying School (aka "Q School"). We weren't going to see each other for two months, but electronic communication was always like a second language for us: We were in touch constantly thanks to Skype, text messages, and e-mail. By the new year it had become clear that our lives were going in different directions, and at the end of January we had the big breakup. I cared about Mark so much I didn't want him to miss out on the chance to have the life he wants. If there had been some infidelity or betrayal, it would've been much easier. If he had been a mooch or a douchebag, that would've been much better. When you break up with someone because you love them, that's when it really hurts.

Ending a relationship via Skype is a pathetic way to do it, and I had to see Mark in person to make it real. That finally happened in Los Angeles, en route to the SBS Open. We had bought our plane tickets long ago, so we stuck to the original plan, meeting up at LAX and then staying at a hotel near the airport. We talked and cried all night, but for all the emotion that poured out, nothing could undo our decision.

Whatever ups and downs I've had in my personal life, golf has always been my sanctuary. It's what I turn to in my times of need. But now golf was what was keeping me apart from an important person in my life. During the practice days in Hawaii, I spent a lot of time trying to get my head around this new reality. I concluded that the one good thing about suddenly being single is that it would allow me to focus all of my energy on achieving the really lofty goals I had set for the season: winning at least two tournaments, contending at multiple major championships, and qualifying for the Solheim Cup, the biennial grudge match between the United States and Europe. Golf was my life before I met Mark, and it showed in my results: I was the youngest player ever to earn a million dollars on the LPGA Tour, and before my twenty-second birthday I had won two tournaments and starred at the Solheim Cup. Having a serious boyfriend gave me a richer, fuller life, but if I'm honest with myself, there were times when golf wasn't my priority, and over the last few years I had been surpassed by a bunch of broads who don't have more talent than I do but were definitely a lot more focused. The breakup meant a fresh start, and now more than ever I was determined to finally realize my potential as a player. That was the plan, anyway.

On the morning of the first round of the SBS, I awoke feeling more settled. The familiar rhythms and routines of a tournament week had helped me take my mind off the now ex-bf, and I was anxious to get out and play. Turtle Bay is one of the best tracks we visit all year—it used to host a Senior Tour event, and it's no accident that a Hall of Famer like Hale Irwin won there six times in a row. I was probably trying a little too hard during an uneven front nine as I made three bogeys that offset three birdies, turning in even par. The eleventh hole is the toughest par-4 on the course but I hit a big drive and made a rock-solid par, giving me a little shot of confidence stepping to the tee of the 490-yard par-5 twelfth. After ripping a drive down the middle, I had 231 yards to the hole. It was a dangerous shot, with water down the left side protecting the green, but of course I was going to go for it. I like to attack a golf course, and par-5s are where I usually do a lot of my damage.

Unfortunately, I hooked my 3-wood and my ball skittered into the hazard short and left of the green. I caught a lucky break, or so it seemed, because the ball was sitting up beautifully on a patch of grass within the hazard. But to play it I had to stand on muddy, rocky earth, with water lapping at my heels. The ball was about eighteen inches above my feet, making the shot that much dicier. Still, I never considered not giving it a whack, because I was confident I could nudge the ball onto the green and give myself a look at birdie. I took a big swing and my club went right underneath the ball. The only direction it moved was straight down.

At that point my caddie, Danny Wilson, said, "You know, you can take a drop."

I wish he had just ripped the club out of my hands because I can be pretty pigheaded, and this time I ignored Danny's advice. Since my ball was now sitting down, I figured making the same swing should result in pretty solid contact. Didn't happen. The grass behind the ball was so thick I stubbed my club in the turf. My ball was just sitting there in the same exact position, mocking me. I finally decided to take a penalty drop outside of the hazard, now my fifth stroke on the hole. I was so mad I was seeing scarlet. If I had taken a drop after my second shot I could have saved par. Now I had to get up and down for double bogey. A so-so pitch left me fifteen feet past the flag, and the downhill putt inexplicably came up a foot short. That's 8 the easy way. Triple bogey.

It's always awkward to watch someone screw up a hole like

that, and my caddie and playing partners were dead quiet on the long walk to the next tee. Finally one of my playing partners, Wendy Ward, said "C'mon, it's all right, get it going." Hearing that made my eyes well up with tears. Some of it was just anger and frustration, but I was also touched by what a big heart Wendy has. How many players would say something like that to someone they're competing against? Not many.

I pride myself on never quitting on a round, and on the thirteenth tee I told Danny, "I'm gonna get my bitch ass back to level par." I hit a good tee shot at thirteen, a really tough uphill par-3, to make a much-needed par, then followed with back-to-back birdies. I could tell Danny was proud of me, and that helped me to keep fighting.

After a series of solid pars I was only one over par on my round arriving at the 399-yard par-4 seventeenth, Turtle Bay's signature hole. It plays out to the ocean with a fairway dotted by nine huge, craggy bunkers. It's a gorgeous enough hole to have been used as a backdrop on *Lost* for the golf match during which Sayid pops a cap in the mysterious character known only as Mr. Avellino. As photogenic as the hole may be, most players on tour would be happy if the course designers dynamited it and started over. The seventeenth always plays dead downwind, the elevated green is so exposed it gets parched and crusty, and there are very few fair pin positions. I busted a 280-yard drive and had only 115 left, but there was no way to stop the ball near the pin, which was only six yards from the front of the green. My ball rolled thirty feet past, leaving a terrifying putt that was downhill and downgrain. I babied the putt, leaving it three and a half feet short, a left-to-right slider with two cups of break. I was so pissed off—at the hole and myself. I was slapping my putter and my thigh over and over again, muttering, "What the hell are you doing? How could you be so stupid?" Having completely lost my composure, I proceeded to miss the par putt, taking a killer bogey. It was so deflating; I had been grinding to salvage my round, slowly getting back near par, and now I was giving it away at the end. Naturally, I failed to birdie the par-5 eighteenth, leaving me in sixty-ninth place with a 74. So much for fresh starts.

The first tournament of the year is like the opening day of a new school year, and there is always a lot to catch up on—who has cute new clothes, whose boobs have grown, who broke up with whom. This time around, there was more talk about business matters. One thing that was immediately evident at the SBS was how many players were "naked," which is to say, lacking endorsement logos on their hats or bags or clothing. The imploding economy was already being felt on tour. There were also a lot of new faces to get to know, as we had a very strong crop of rookies. Every year the entourages seem to grow, and the range was shoulder to shoulder with unfamiliar swing coaches, parents, caddies, agents, trainers, short-game instructors, boyfriends, girlfriends, and all manner of hangers-on. Even though I was still only twenty-four, this was my seventh year on tour, and not knowing so many of the newbies made me feel old and a little disoriented.

My split with Mark wasn't the only news when it came to the tour's dating scene. The juiciest breakup involved a player and a female caddie who had split after the player spent the off-season cavorting in Europe with other women. The caddie was so devastated, she was taking a year off to sort things out emotionally. Needless to say, romance on tour can be quite complicated, and I think that's why all the other players had been so supportive of my relationship with Mark. They know it's not easy to get laid on the LPGA Tour. We're like a traveling circus that barnstorms in and out of a new town every week, and this vagabond lifestyle makes it hard to meet quality people or get serious with those you do come across. If one of the guys on the PGA Tour is feeling lonely, there is always a nice selection of so-called rope hopers, those pretty young things who show up at tournaments in short skirts and do-me heels and preen by the gallery ropes, hoping to attract a wandering eye. Even if you are so inclined, it's slim pickings in our galleries: horny teens clutching Natalie Gulbis calendars, dads with their daughters, or retirees in sandals with black socks. Given that a lot of girls are not getting much action, I'm sure the average golf fan would be shocked to know how much we talk about sex during tournament rounds. Once I was paired with a good friend who regaled me with stories from this raunchy book she was reading, *I Hope They Serve Beer in Hell*, in which a real-life cad recounts his various sexual misadventures. All of the fans who saw us in rapt conversation probably assumed we were discussing the finer points of Mickey Wright's swing or Alister MacKenzie's bunkering, but really it was naughty sex talk the whole time.

I was lucky to meet a nice guy like Mark, but more than a few caddies get lucky just because they're there. (Suggested title for a future LPGA movie: *Caddyshag*.) At least half a dozen players on tour have married caddies, but it can be a complicated arrangement, especially if you spend all day together on the golf course. Not long ago I was staying in a hotel room across the hall from a player who employs her husband as a caddie. Walking to my room I could hear shouting coming from theirs. Naturally, I did what anybody would do: pretend to be looking for my key so I could stand in the hall and eavesdrop. Apparently they had just finished a bad round, and the player was saying, "All I wanted was for you to be there for me. All I wanted was for you to pat me on the back and say you're proud of me."

The poor guy was sobbing, saying, "I gave up my whole life for you."

"What life? You didn't have a life."

It was pretty heavy.

Mark actually caddied for me a few times in our first months of dating, and it was definitely a different vibe. He was trying to keep it professional, but I kept saying things like, "Hey, I think I'm gonna hit my ball into the woods so we can go look for it, wink wink."

If you are a player in need of loving and want to avoid caddie entanglements, then another option is the agents and equipment reps who service the tour. These guys aren't out on tour every week like the caddies, so there is a little air of mystery, and they're usually not as sweaty, which is a plus. Some of them definitely get passed around, and one swordsman among them was particularly notorious. You know how Picasso had his Blue Period, then his Rose Period, and so on? This one agent had his cougar period, during which he nailed an Aussie who was a big deal about a quarter century ago. This was followed by an Asian period, and then he moved on to Europeans, eventually marrying one. If my math is correct, all the players this guy shagged have won a total of eighteen major championships. Hey, he's tied with Jack Nicklaus!

I had an early tee time for my second round at the SBS and was looking forward to calmer conditions so I could post a low score and get back in the tournament. No such luck—the wind was howling when I got to the golf course. I hit a bad opening tee shot and nothing went right from there. I bogeyed three of the first four holes and it was a death march the rest of the way. I was feeling so out of it mentally, making bad decision after bad decision; it wasn't until later that I realized how emotionally spent I was from all the breakup drama. I was still three over par playing my final hole, the birdie-able par-5 ninth. Of course it started raining sideways as I was in the fairway, and the wind knocked my third shot left of the green. From there I made an ugly bogey to finish off a 76. I thought that final bogey would ensure a missed cut, so I was steaming as I walked off the course. Little did I know things were about to get worse.

After signing my scorecard, I was confronted by an LPGA official who officiously informed me that I was being fined $2,500 because the day before I had been quoted using the f-word in a British fish wrap called the *Guardian*. The story behind the story: Earlier in the week I had been approached by an unfamiliar reporter for an interview about Michelle Wie, who was the big attraction coming into the SBS because she was making her debut as a tour member on the island where she had grown up. I had plenty to say about Michelle because we're good friends, and I have always been protective of her in a big-sisterly way. We first met at the 2003 Kraft Nabisco Championship, when we were paired together for the first two rounds. She was a hotshot thirteen-year-old who blew in with a ton of hype and had to deal with the inevitable jealousy from many of the other players. But I welcomed her with open arms and basically said, Hey, if you can kick all of our butts, then good for you, go do it. We clicked because we had a lot in common: Both of us had turned pro in our teens and were raised in the U.S. by traditional Korean parents, leading to similar pressures on the home front. And Michelle has always liked that I don't scare easily and can say things she only wishes she could. So when the bloke with the notebook asked me about Michelle's many critics, I had a snappy response: "Fuck the naysayers."

As soon as it came out of my mouth I realized it was a mistake. I asked the reporter if we could amend the quote, and after some back and forth he came up with "Snuff the naysayers." We parted ways and I never thought twice about the interview until I was informed of my fine. As soon as that conversation ended I marched to the media center. The offending scribe was lucky that he had already fled Hawaii, but I obtained his e-mail address and immediately dashed off a nasty note. He replied that after our conversation he had thought further about how to handle the quote and, after consulting with his editor, decided it was not his responsibility to edit my language.

My knee-jerk reaction was to appeal the fine. I was certainly familiar with that process, as over my career I had already been fined many thousands of dollars for my on-course language. (That represents a lot of transgressions. In a given season you are dinged one hundred dollars for the first offense, two hundred for the second, five hundred for the third, and one thousand thereafter.) But what can I say? I'm a passionate, emotive player, and sometimes things just kind of slip out. I blame it on Dottie Pepper. I followed her at the very first tournament I ever attended as a kid, and after every bad shot she would scream, "Dammit, Dottie!" I remember thinking how cool it was that on the LPGA the players could utter whatever oaths they chose. Turns out that's not the case. At the 2008 Stanford International Pro-Am, I hit a bad shot and my involuntary reaction was to yell, "Goddammit!" I tried to catch myself and wound up saying something that sounded like "Gaught dane it!" When I was informed of a thousand-dollar fine, I argued that what came out of my mouth weren't even actual words. The LPGA official to whom I stated my case was unmoved and the fine stood. I remember thinking, *Great, now I'm getting fined just for the intent of saying something inappropriate!*

Upon further reflection, I decided not to appeal the f-bomb fine. I don't want to be uncouth or crass. Whatever the extenuating circumstance, my profanity was printed, simple as that. It's not cool if the LPGA loses even one fan because I've offended them. And beginning with the SBS Open, I needed to hold myself to a higher standard because I was now a member of the LPGA's player-director board. I had been elected on Monday of tournament week during a mandatory player meeting. I had actually run twice before in previous years but lost to other players in a vote of the membership. It was so embarrassing to lose those elections but I love the LPGA and want to help steer it in a positive direction, so I decided to run one more time. It looked like I was going to be unopposed, but at the meeting another player nominated herself to the ballot. My heart sank because she's a glamorous former major championship winner. It took me right back to when I ran for treasurer in eighth grade, that feeling of *Oh no, she's so much prettier than I am so there's no way I can win*. At the meeting, votes were taken on little ballots and tour officials quickly tabulated the results. When it was announced that I had won there was much clapping and high-fiving and I screamed the only thing that seemed appropriate: "I'm going to Disneyland!"

As it turned out, the afternoon scores from the second round came in higher than expected—thank you, wind—and I wound up making the cut on the number. I was happy to have eighteen more holes to try to find my game. I started the final round strong with three birdies on the outward nine, but my on-course malaise returned in the form of three bogeys over the final five holes for a 73 that left me in fiftieth place. For my efforts I earned $3,914. Given the cost of airfare, hotel, food, and caddie fees, plus my fine, I was definitely going to lose money on the week. But in a weird way it was a very rewarding tournament. The whole week was such a challenge. I learned from it, I kept clawing, and in the end I prevailed over a lot of adversity just by virtue of not throwing myself into the Pacific.

After my final round was over I made a point of watching the finish on TV, something I rarely do. It was pretty thrilling stuff. Michelle Wie played awesome on the front nine and held a two-stroke lead at the turn but was run down on the closing holes thanks to a birdie binge by Angela Stanford, one of the tour's emerging stars. I wasn't the only one

watching—thanks to Michelle, the final round drew huge rat-
ings on the Golf Channel, and lpga.com had one of its busiest
weeks ever. I've been saying for a while that Michelle is going
to be one of the best things that's ever happened to the LPGA.
She's intelligent, she's beautiful, she's witty, she's six feet tall,
and she just has that star quality that makes her impossible to
ignore. Even though golfers are selfish by nature, I think everyone else finally understood that what Michelle did was great
for the tour and that she would be bringing plenty of buzz to
the rest of the season. Michelle had earned a lot of respect by
swallowing her pride and going through Q School, and I think
at the SBS the attitude toward her was, You've gotten all the
hype, now bring it. And she brought it.

Proving the golf gods have a sense of humor, the final round
of the SBS fell on Valentine's Day. The LPGA is the death of
holidays. I always loved Halloween, but now we're always at a
tournament in Japan or Korea and it's no fun to celebrate over
there. For Valentine's we're either playing a tournament or on
a plane home. With so many girls alone on V-Day, there was
a certain sadness and resignation in the air, but no one organized a pathetic group ice cream binge or anything like that.
It's just part of the life and you have to accept it.

I happened to be one of the few girls with Valentine's Day
plans. Mark and I had bumped into each other a few times
during the week—in our cloistered little world, it was impossible not to—and we were determined to try to remain friends.
Since neither of us had anything better to do, we decided to
go out for a V-Day dinner. For the occasion I squeezed into a
low-cut dress that showed off the twins. I wasn't hoping for
make up sex, but I did want to look good for Mark, just out of

habit. The date turned out to be a disaster. The whole evening was awkward and just made me even sadder about the demise of what we once had.

Having a bad Valentine's Day was the perfect end to my week. Hawaii is such a paradise, but this time I couldn't wait to get the hell off that island. It was only the first tournament and it had already been a long year.

CHAPTER 2

Daddy's Girl

Following Hawaii, there was a week off before our next tournament in Thailand. It didn't make sense to fly all the way home to Orlando, so I decided to spend the week in the desert, working on my game and repairing my relationship with the most important person in my life: my father, Man Kim. After playing eighteen holes at Mission Hills Country Club in Palm Springs, site of the upcoming Dinah Shore, I drove on to Phoenix. Dad had flown in earlier from the house I share with my parents in Orlando and was waiting when I arrived. Wrapping me in a big bear hug, he whispered, "I missed you." I had missed him, too, for the better part of three years.

My relationship with my parents changed dramatically when I began dating Mark. They hated him and wouldn't deign to acknowledge his existence even if he walked into the same room. I don't think it was personal—I was their little girl, he was my first boyfriend (that they knew about!), and whoever he was, he wasn't going to be good enough for them.

(Though being a caddie and not a doctor certainly didn't help Mark's cause.) When I reached the LPGA in 2003 I was the youngest player on tour at eighteen, and my dad took on an all-encompassing role. I called him "Cocamadaddy" to reflect his hybrid position of coach, caddie, manager, and father. My mom, Dianna, traveled with us to nearly every tournament, and we were a very tight, insular family unit. That changed when I got with Mark, and to protect us from my parents' hostility I became defiant and increasingly reduced their role in my life. The same year I met Mark, my dad was relieved of his caddying duties and I hired an agent. Instead of hovering over my every swing, my parents gradually stopped coming to all but a few tournaments. I needed the space to become my own woman, but it was very painful for all of us to grow apart, especially me and the old man. I had always been Daddy's little girl and thought I would be forever.

Needless to say, my parents were thrilled when Mark and I broke up. Before leaving for Hawaii, I was moping around the house in Orlando and Dad kept saying in his charmingly imperfect English, "Why you so sad? Best thing ever happen in your life!"

When I got to Phoenix, my dad could see I was still hurting and he was more comforting, but neither of us really wanted to talk about my love life. There was golf to be played. The annual tour stop in Phoenix, to be played four weeks after Thailand, was moving to a new muni named Papago, and I teed it up there six times in four days, a sort of cart polo in which I would be sent off in the first group every morning and complete eighteen holes in under two hours. (The afternoon rounds, with the paying riffraff, took more like five hours.) My dad rode shotgun for every shot. We had a blast just being together and bonding again on a golf course, then talking about my game over long, relaxing dinners.

Scoping out new venues has been a tradition of ours going back to November 2002, prior to my rookie year, when my parents and I crisscrossed the country in a sagging 1995 Dodge van, visiting twenty-one courses on the upcoming LPGA schedule. Twice I got snowed on, including a round at Wykagyl Country Club outside New York City when I kept losing my ball in the three inches of powder. It was a little madcap, but my dad insisted I play on. He has always wanted to give me every opportunity to succeed. Like many girls on tour—and just about all those of Korean ancestry—my dad was the driving force in my career from the very beginning.

Growing up in San Jose, California, I used to love weekend mornings because my mom would always get up early to cook pancakes and our whole house had the wondrous smell of melted butter and warm syrup. Even though we were the only Koreans in the neighborhood, I liked to imagine that we were the perfect American family enjoying a perfect American breakfast. At some point when I was eleven, the pancakes abruptly stopped coming and I would stumble out of bed to a cold and dark and lonely household. My brother and sister and I had no idea where our parents were or what they were doing, only that hours later they would come home jaunty and sun-kissed, pretending nothing was amiss. Turns out they were sneaking off to a nearby golf course to tee it up with friends who had introduced them to the game. One day Dad turned up with a funny-looking metal stick with a bulbous end. Marching me to the backyard, he threw down a strip of Astroturf and grunted, "Here, swing hard as you can." I did, and it was kind of fun. Then he told me to do it 499 more times. This was my introduction to a golf club and the golf swing. Being a dutiful Korean daughter, I never thought to question my dad, and every day after school I would spend two hours making the required five hundred swings, as would my older brother, Mel, and older sister, Gloria.

After a month of this tedium, Dad finally took us to a driving range so we could hit actual golf balls and watch them fly. It was like the clouds parted and the angels were singing and I finally understood there was a point to all of this. I quickly became immersed in competitive golf on the Junior Golf Association of Northern California circuit.

One thing I loved about golf from the beginning was that it was a way to get my parents' attention. As the runt of the litter, I crave attention. I chug it. So when it came to golf, I was kind of like the teacher's pet. Mel is the most naturally talented player I've ever seen, but he had a hard time dealing with Dad's exacting standards. Free spirit that he is, Mel quit playing competitive golf at eighteen and became an accordion-playing surf bum. (You can imagine how thrilled my parents were.) Gloria tried harder, but she never quite fell in love with golf and she, too, gave it up at eighteen. So by my midteens I was the family's only shot at golf glory. In the beginning I had played just to make my parents happy, but when I was fifteen the desire to excel became like a fire burning inside of me. The spark was the Sacramento city junior championship, at which I shot 70 at Hagen Oaks Golf Course, my first time breaking par. (My official score was 72 because of a two-stroke penalty for arriving a few minutes late to my tee time, but never mind.) I've always been an all-or-nothing kind of personality, and the more I poured myself into golf the better I played, which only made me want to try that much harder. I also liked how golf made me feel about myself. I've always been a little self-conscious about my size—I was five foot six in the third grade, and definitely not shaped like California Barbie. Thanks to all of my backyard work I was a solid ball striker from the beginning, and launching 240-yard drives made me feel powerful and confident.

Back in Korea my dad had studied kinesiology, and he later taught physical education at the high school level. He took a very analytical approach to my golf development: During tournaments he would clamor through the trees like a descendant of Bigfoot, schlepping an oversized video camera . . . with a tripod. In those days no other parents were taping their daughter's rounds, and I was totally mortified by my dad and his omnipresent camera. But there's no denying the guy's dedication. One year I played a tournament in Humboldt County, way up in the northern end of the state. We got up at three A.M., drove seven hours in our rickety '89 Oldsmobile, played one round, and then drove home, arriving around midnight. It wasn't until later in life that I discovered what the inside of a hotel room looked like.

I kept playing tournament golf and had some nice success, including my first national victory at the 2000 High School Open Championship and qualifying for the match-play portion of the U.S. Women's Amateur later that summer. So at the end of 2000, when I was sixteen, I made one of the biggest decisions of my life: to leave Oak Grove High School and focus on golf full-time. Everybody assumed my dad had forced me to do it, but it was completely my decision. My parents really weren't for it or against it, but they knew there was no way they could change my mind, so they gave me their blessing. I aced the California State Equivalency Exam, giving me the status of a high school graduate, which was fine for my mom and dad. People think Korean parents are obsessed with education, but from what I've seen all they really care about is achievement, and schooling is merely a means to an end. I had been a straight-A student my entire life, and by junior high often found myself bored during class. As my commitment to golf deepened, I would often think, "The sun is shining, so why am I sitting inside studying what I already know? I should be out there hitting balls!" Some of my high school friends were baffled by my decision and a common sentiment was, Oh, no, but you'll miss the prom! For me it was simple— did I want to be groped by some kid with bad breath and backne, or did I want to be serenaded by thousands of fans at the U.S. Women's Open in faraway and exotic (to me) North Carolina? On prom weekend I finished forty-eighth at my first Open and never looked back.

That summer of 2001, when I was seventeen, was when I realized I could compete with the best players in the country. The breakthrough came at the U.S. Girls' Junior. I shot a 62 during the stroke-play qualifying, the lowest score any player, male or female, had ever shot in the history of the United States Golf Association, which began conducting tournaments in 1895. (In 2006 Billy Horschel broke my record with a 60 in the first round of the U.S. Amateur. Jerk.) We never had enough money to travel to the big-time amateur events, so I really didn't have any concept of what a big deal the U.S. Junior was, although I got an inkling with all the media attention that accompanied my 62. (Sample headline, which gently mocked my goofy postround interview: RECORDS SHATTERED AS TEENAGER KIM CARDS "CELESTIAL" 62.) I just went out and played with a purity and innocence and insouciance I wish I could recapture.

To keep pushing myself, I spent the rest of that summer competing as an amateur on the Futures Tour, the primary minor league circuit for women's golf. I knew I was good enough to play professionally when I reached a play-off in my first start, and I wound up making the cut in all eight events and enjoying two other top-ten finishes against deep fields of grizzled journeywomen and recent grads from big-time college programs. Due to LPGA bylaws, I had to wait until my eighteenth birthday to turn pro, so on March 15, 2002, I made it official. Honestly, it was pretty anticlimactic. In fact, it was pathetic. I was riding in a golf cart with my dad when I realized the time had arrived. So I said, "Hey, Dad, guess what? I'm a pro!" We did a little high five and that was it.

I competed on the Futures the rest of that year and played quite well from start to finish. The highlight was something called the Hewlett-Packard Garden State Futures Golf Classic, which I won in a play-off against a little pixie named Lorena Ochoa, who had just finished setting a million records at the University of Arizona. Lorena and I spent the rest of the season trading the top spot on the Futures Tour money list. Naturally it came down to the last hole of the last round of the last tournament, in York, Pennsylvania. I played the par-4 eighteenth knowing a birdie would give me the money title and a lifetime of bragging rights with Lorena. I hit a clutch approach

shot to three feet. Unfortunately, on the Futures Tour the
course conditions can be a little spotty, and it looked like there
was a demilitarized zone between my ball and the hole. I was
just trying to bank the putt off a couple spike marks, curve it
through a little dead patch, and get the right bounce off a dan-
delion. It didn't happen. The putt lipped out and I lost the
money title by all of $242. (I still pocketed $53,600 for the season, way more than any of my friends were making flipping
burgers back in San Jose.) The big consolation was that the top
three finishers on the money list earned a spot on the LPGA
Tour for the upcoming 2003 season. I was headed to the big
leagues, doe-eyed and dipshitted.

The first tournament of my rookie year was the Welch's/Fry's
Championship in Tucson, Arizona. I believed in my talent
but I had so much to learn about playing golf at that level. My
playing partner was Dina Ammaccapane, a longtime veteran
on tour, and on the first hole we both missed the green short.
Dina was away and hit this awesome flop shot to two feet. I
thought it was such a cool play I wanted to try it, too. A more
prudent touring pro might have spent a few weeks perfect-
ing the shot on a practice green, but I gave it a go right then
and there. Not a great idea. I flubbed my flop twenty-five feet
past the hole. I was so embarrassed; my dad, who was doubling
as my caddie, gave me a nasty look and was muttering something in Korean under his breath. But I drained the putt to
save par and was off and running, shooting a spiffy 64. I backed
that up with a 67, setting up a magical third round.

   When I arrived on the first tee, the crowd launched into a

rousing rendition of "Happy Birthday." It was so touching I almost cried. Being such a rube, I was like, How did they know? It never occurred to me that the newspaper accounts that morning mentioned that I was turning nineteen.

I don't know if the birthday cheer was responsible, but I played almost perfect golf that day, making eight birdies against no bogeys at Dell Ulrich Golf Course. My 62 could have been even lower but for three birdie putts that spun out. After my round I was ushered into the media center for my first-ever press conference. I thrived on the attention. Maybe they were just delighted that I wasn't a stereotypical quiet Korean, but all the middle-aged white guys with notebooks seemed to love my shtick. I became an instant media darling, at least according to the local paper, and I've tried to live up to that ever since. I also wasted no time making myself known to the other players. On the tenth hole I thought I'd mis-hit my approach shot and blurted out, "Oh crap!" This was picked up by the TV cameras, as was my revisionist reaction after the shot took a lucky bounce and wound up a foot from the hole: "Never mind." Almost instantly other players began greeting me with, "Ohcrapnevermind."

All week long I had been so carefree, but the nerves hit me big-time on Sunday, when I was in the final group alongside Lorie Kane, who had won four times in the preceding couple of years. Lorie is one of the nicest human beings on the planet, and she was so good to my dad and me that day, gently educating us on where to stand, where he should put the golf bag so as not to distract the other players, and a lot of other nuances about which we were totally clueless. I got off to too good a start, birdying the first two holes. Arriving on the third tee, I was leading the tournament and I started freaking out. I was having trouble breathing properly, and it was like all the feeling had left my hands and arms. I stopped swinging as aggressively, and the result was that I didn't have nearly as many birdie opportunities the rest of the way. Still, I wound up holding it together for an even-par 70, tying for fourth, five strokes behind winner Karen Stupples. Of course I would have loved to have won, but I wasn't ready for that yet, at least mentally. Still, I was pretty thrilled with my first week on tour. Others took notice, too: *Sports Illustrated* called it "one of the most audacious debuts in LPGA history."

Things did not go nearly as smoothly the rest of the season, as I had only one more top-ten finish, but it was a year of tremendous personal growth. Even though I was born in the U.S. I had a pretty traditional Korean upbringing, which had left me deferential and reserved. During my school years I had plenty of friends, but I always felt a little different because of the whole golf thing. On the LPGA I was suddenly surrounded by young women who shared my passion and dreams, and amongst these peers I blossomed. People began to comment that my dad was much more "Korean" than I was. My individuality began to be expressed in my on-course look.

A surprising number of golfers listen to hip-hop—hell, even Juli Inkster, a fortysomething mother of two, has been known to bump some rap music. But I was the first player to appropriate the fashion. The pimpish Kangol hats popularized by LL Cool J back in the day became my trademark. During my rookie year I bought one in every color to go along with the ever-changing tints in my hair. I also began shopping for clothes at the wannabe death-metal store at a mall in San Jose.

In 2003 there were five other players on tour named Kim—now there are a dozen—but I'm pretty sure none of them have ever been confused for me. My dad wanted me to dress in more boring, traditional golf attire, and would occasionally suggest some hideous matronly outfit. My standard reply: "The only way I'm wearing that is if I die and you get to dress me for the funeral."

Clothing was not the only source of contention. The player-caddie dynamic is delicate enough without the accumulated baggage of a crosscultural, multigenerational father-daughter relationship. My parents were both traveling with me full-time, and some of the tension would come out between the ropes. Of my dad and me, tour veteran Grace Park once told a reporter, "They are always pecking at each other. He'll say things to her that I would never take from my caddie. I mean, he'd be gone that second. But she gives it right back."

Things reached a boiling point early in the 2004 season, my sophomore year on tour. My dad and I were really going at it on the course and we finally did some heavy-duty soul-searching in the weeks before the Kraft Nabisco Championship. When we arrived there he told me he was going to back off, that from now on he would let me call the shots on the course. Hearing that relaxed me so much: I suddenly felt that if I made a mistake I would only be letting myself down, not him, too. A defining moment for us came during the third round of the Kraft. I was sneaking up the leaderboard as I played the par-5 eighteenth hole, which has an island green. After busting a 290-yard drive I was 214 yards from the hole and stewing on whether or not to go for it. Dad put down the bag and said, "Don't look at me, it's your decision." I had never attempted to reach the green in two, even in a practice round, but then again, I had never bombed such a perfect drive. When I pulled out my 5-wood, my dad walked away and turned his back—he couldn't bear to watch. But I ripped a hard draw that cleared the water by a couple of yards, and my ball nestled in the center of the green for an eagle opportunity, inspiring Dad to sprint across the fairway for a hug and a series of knuckle bumps. Looking back, that one shot was crucial in my development as a player. Three months later I won my first tournament, the Longs Drugs Challenge, surviving a Sunday dogfight against two Hall of Famers, Inkster and Karrie Webb. (I wound up birdying five of the last eight holes for a closing 65.)

After the final putt dropped, clinching my victory, I collapsed into my dad's arms on the green. He was holding me so tight and we were both crying uncontrollably. It was such an emotional moment, I still choke up when thinking about it.

I won again in 2005, and that year I also went 2-1-1 to help the United States take the Solheim Cup. Still only twenty-one, I thought I was going to be the next Annika, but I didn't count on a big distraction that would come into my life. How big? Oh, about five foot eleven. Fast-forward three years, and now that Mark was out of the picture I felt like I was going back to basics with my golf.

My dad has always been my only instructor. During our four days in Phoenix at Papago I played great as he told me what he always tells me: "Swing hard and stop talking so much." Finally, it was time for me to fly to Bangkok for the second tournament of the 2009 season, the Honda LPGA Thailand. Dad drove me to Los Angeles, and just like in the old days we passed the time by kibitzing and scanning the horizon for cop cars.

Upon reaching L.A., we swung by Whole Foods so I could pick up some necessities for any overseas trip: two boxes of Cliff bars, a bottle of amino acids to combat dehydration, a Sharpie for signing autographs, three jugs of SPF 70 sunblock, and eucalyptus and peppermint oil to burn so my hotel rooms would feel more spalike. Dropping me at the airport, my dad gave me another big hug. "Play your best," he said. I've always played for myself, but making my dad proud is definitely a strong motivation. I thought about that as I watched him drive away.

For every limited-field international event, the players' airfare and accommodations are paid for by the tournament, an inducement for us to make the long, tiring trips. On the flight to Bangkok there were a dozen of us girls in business class, and it was like a party in the pointy end of the airplane, with people swapping seats to chat and sharing snacks and DVDs. Upon arrival we were put up at a five-star resort in the town of Chonburi, about an hour southeast of Bangkok. We were obviously well taken care of, but Thailand still left me with a funny feeling. Everywhere I went there were gross middle-aged white guys walking around with very young Thais on their arm. Sometimes they were girls, sometimes boys, and occasionally they were the so-called ladyboys, men in drag. Whatever the tastes of these lascivious tourists, I found it totally creepy.

I practiced hard in the days before the tournament, but did make time for a little shopping. There is knockoff everything available in Thailand, and I actually enjoy the haggling that is an inevitable part of the process. The merchants don't even try to pretend what they're selling is the real thing. One woman was trying to hawk a "Prada" bag, saying, "It good quality, made in Korea." Hello, it's supposed to be Italian.

The Plantation Course at Siam Country Club is a very pretty layout, but I hate the greens. I think whenever an elephant dies in Thailand, they bury it under the Plantation's putting surfaces. The slopes are so extreme they have to keep the greens shaggy to make them playable. So you have very fast putts down the steep slopes, but anything flat or uphill you have to smash to get to the hole. I struggled with the speed throughout the practice rounds and it didn't get better once the tournament began. On the first hole of the first round I left a five-footer for par about a foot short. Nice. On the second hole my approach with a sand wedge flew a little too long and I was left with an impossible downhill putt. I three-putted for another bogey.

Sometimes a bad start can ruin my whole round, but I was determined to grind out a good score, even after more putting problems led to bogeys at eight and nine. I played the back nine in two under to finish with an even-par 72. Playing overseas can sometimes pose unique challenges, and I was reminded of that during the first round. On the par-3 sixteenth hole there was a local photographer who obviously knew nothing about golf. The experienced snappers never take pictures until a player's follow-through, so as not to be a distraction. This jackass in Thailand stood near the tee box, clicking the whole way through my swing. The sound of the camera firing definitely made me flinch. While I was still finishing my swing I yelled at him, "Oh no you didn't!" He started walking away, so I chased after him. (As it turned out, my shot landed on the green, but that's not the point.) Seeing me coming, he wisely broke into a sprint. I gave up the chase, yelling after him, "Have some etiquette!" I wanted to say something a little stronger but was trying not to get fined again.

The third hole at the Plantation Course is a 182-yard par-3. The second-round pin position was very tricky, in the back middle, on the crown of a big hump. If you didn't favor the right side of the green your tee shot would funnel left, off the putting surface and into a collection area. Naturally, I pulled my tee shot dead at the flag and it kicked left into the swale. That gave me a delicate chip, which I flew about one yard too far. It raced past the hole and all the way off the other side of the green. Now I faced another nasty little shot, back up the steep slope. I put too much spin on my chip and the ball expired on the hill, rolling back to my feet. My head started to spin. I actually had to count on my fingers how many shots I had taken. Laying three, I now needed to get up and down for double bogey. I benched my 60-degree lob wedge and decided to give my 56-degree sand wedge a try, but I didn't hit the shot quite hard enough, and once again my ball rolled back to my feet. I could feel my cheeks flush, and now I became aware that the group behind us was loitering on the tee box, waiting for their turn as they watched my train wreck unfold. A sense of panic washed over me—I may never leave this hole! I capitulated and played away from the flag to the center of the green. From forty feet I two-putted for a quadruple-bogey 7. You know when you're not wearing underwear and your skirt rips down the middle? That's how mortified I was. My playing partner Karen Stupples tried to be helpful by saying, "Hey, you have fifteen holes left."

"Don't fucking remind me," I muttered.

Karen wouldn't quit. "That's fifteen chances at birdie. Play hard."

I always put a ton of pressure on myself about results, which dates back to my junior golf days when my dad had such high expectations for me. Some players can lose themselves in the process, just hit one shot at a time, and not worry about the outcome. Before a tournament even begins I'm stressing about where I'll finish. In a weird way making that 7 freed me up to just go play and not worry about my score, because it felt like I had already ruined the round.

On the next hole I hooked my drive so far left I couldn't see the flag for my approach shot, but my caddie Danny figured out the yardage and gave me a very helpful aiming point. I stuck a 9-iron to twelve feet and after I poured in the birdie putt, Danny gave me a fist pump. It was kind of goofy, but his enthusiasm helped get me going. The fifth hole is a high-risk/high-reward par-4 of about 270 yards; since I had nothing to lose, I tried to drive the green. My tee shot flew into a greenside bunker, but I got up and down for another birdie. My scorecard was clean for the rest of the round, twelve pars and one more birdie for a 74. All things considered, it was a pretty decent score.

After every round I call my dad, sometimes within seconds of walking off the eighteenth hole. He religiously follows my scores on the Internet but is always dying for the play-by-play. This time when I called him the first thing he blurted out was, "What happened?!" I didn't have to ask what he was referring to.

In the third round I got off to a nice start for a change, but then I lost the feel for my wedges. I was having trouble hitting them the correct distances, and that contributed to bogeys on five of my last ten holes, en route to a dispiriting 76. This time I was in tears when I called my dad. When I make mistakes on the golf course I have to put the emotion aside and keep playing, and the feelings just get bottled up. But I'm a girl, and sooner or later all that emotion has to pour out; it usually happens when I'm talking to Dad. Not that he's ever warm and fuzzy on the phone.

"How can you make bogey on par five? On *reachable* par five? Do you know people are shooting six under?"

"Uh, yeah, there are scoreboards here in Thailand. I don't really want . . ."

"No, you need to hear this. I know you can win, I know you can be number one. Play better!"

It sounds harsh, but he means well. Dad believes in my talent so much that he just doesn't comprehend when I play poorly. Yes, he could express this a little more delicately, but talking to him almost always makes me feel better, and on the occasions when I break down and cry I usually play with more resolve the next day. For the final round in Thailand I bogeyed the first hole for the third time that week, but I just shrugged it off and played great the rest of the way, firing a 69 that was easily my best round of the year so far. That moved me up to thirty-fourth place, worth $10,209.

Of course, I may have had such a good attitude because of the elephant ride scheduled for after the round. I was excited all day, telling the other players, "I'm going to wrap my thighs around a big, smelly beast—I haven't done that in a few months!" Giulia Sergas, a tour veteran by way of Italy, came with me to this lush, forested area about fifteen minutes from the course. We brought three bunches of bananas for the elephants and they ate them out of our hands. Then we climbed aboard and went for a long tour of the countryside, the elephants piloted by a guide who would spear them with his bare feet to get them to change directions. At one point we crossed a river that was about eight feet deep and the waterline came just below the elephants' eye level. It was one of the most thrilling things I've ever done.

Whenever the LPGA visits somewhere exotic I try to do something cultural or otherwise indigenous to the area to get a sense of place. This job is an adventure, and you have to embrace it. Otherwise it's a huge drag, an endless procession of golf courses, hotels, airports, and long-distance phone calls. After the elephant ride Giulia and I were still in a daring mood, so we journeyed to the outskirts of Bangkok to the top of a futuristic building that looked a bit like Seattle's Space Needle. From the fifty-seventh floor it was possible to zipline back down to the ground. I don't like heights and was convinced my steel cable was going to snap and I would plummet to earth, popping like a grape on impact. I was nearly dry-heaving by the time my turn came, but it wound up being a pretty smooth ride down. The next time I talked to my dad I made a point to not mention the ziplining.

From Bangkok we flew about eight hundred miles south into Singapore for the HSBC Women's Champions. I was excited, and not just because I had finished eighth there the year before and felt good vibes about the course. Singapore is my favorite city in the world, by far. It is so exotic. The weather is tropical, the food is unique and delicious, and there is amazing nightlife and shopping. And yet you can walk out of the fanciest store or restaurant and see monkeys in the trees and birds of every imaginable color. The city is clean, there's almost no crime, and everyone always seems so happy. It's utopia.

The tournament is also one of the best we play all year, the self-styled "Asian major." HSBC also hosts a men's tournament, so they know how to do it right: We were picked up at the airport in Audis, not packed onto a stinky bus like in Thailand, and then deposited at the Ritz-Carlton. That's how I like to roll.

Tanah Merah Country Club is a great track but the weather didn't cooperate. In the week before the tournament there had been some ten inches of rain, so the greens were not nearly as firm and fast as they'd been in previous years. I had putted so well in 2008 and could never quite make the mental adjustment to the different speed and different breaks. (It didn't help that the practice putting surface was much, much faster than the greens on the course.) I hit the ball nicely during the first round but couldn't score, as again my wedge game was a little off. The disappointment of my one-over-par 73 was leavened by the Jason Mraz concert that night. I've loved his music for years and almost fainted when I discovered he would be in Singapore during the tournament week. IMG was putting on the concert, so I had my friend Morgan Pressel, an IMG client, hook us up with some sweet comped tickets.

How into the concert was I? I took exactly 976 pictures of Jason in less than two hours. Afterward we got to go backstage and meet him. I reverted to a giggly eleven-year-old girl, and I was acting so goofy Morgan threatened to leave. We talked with Jason for about fifteen minutes and he was so dreamy—very cute and spiritual. I think I killed the Zenlike vibe when I asked him to autograph my cleavage, but he obliged. What a sweetheart.

The second and third rounds at the HSBC were eerily like my first. I was swinging well but everything was just a little bit off. I posted two more 73s. Following the last of them I was so frustrated that once again I wound up crying to my dad on the phone.

Over the first sixteen holes of the final round I was spinning my wheels, with fifteen pars and a bogey. Standing on the seventeenth tee I had only one thought: No fucking way am I gonna have to call my dad and explain another 73. I summoned a series of perfect shots, birdying the last two holes for a 71 that moved me to thirty-first place.

That night a few of us went to a packed, sweaty nightclub in the downtown. Angela Park was shaking her little thing, and she may or may not have inspired a couple of HSBC execs to dance on top of a table. Yani Tseng was there too. When she parties, she parties hard. Before she retired, Annika Sorenstam anointed Yani as the next number one, the player most likely to challenge Lorena Ochoa's hegemony. No doubt Yani has the talent, but it will be interesting to see if she has the discipline to get there.

The next day brought the long flight back to the U.S. I spent part of the time reflecting on my play. It had been a pretty frustrating couple of tournaments, but I was buoyed by my final conversation with my dad. With a nod to my closing birdies in Singapore, he told me something that I know is in his heart but he doesn't say out loud very often: "I'm proud of you." Those words carried me home.

CHAPTER 3

South by Southwest

As soon as my flight from Singapore landed in Los Angeles, I rented a car and blazed down the coast to Carlsbad, the little town where almost all of the big equipment manufacturers are based. There was a week off before our next tournament, the MasterCard Classic in Mexico City, and my sticks needed some serious tweaking.

The problems had begun in January, long before the real season started, when I traveled to Rio de Janeiro for an unofficial tournament. As I grabbed my travel bag at the airport, it bent at a weird angle and I got a sick feeling in my stomach. Sure enough, my driver shaft had snapped in transit. I was utterly devastated. Understand, this was no ordinary club. This driver had been my steady since November 2006, one of the longest committed relationships of my life. It was a Callaway FT-3 with the hottest face I had ever hit, and in 2007 I used it to bash my way to ninth in the LPGA's driving-distance stats, at 264.9 yards a pop. And the club kept working: I finished sixteenth in '08. I tried to have an identical club built as a backup, but Callaway could never come up with one that felt right. I don't know if it was the way the epoxy dried on my gamer or if the moon was in the house of Libra when it was built or if it was all in my head, but I could never find another one I liked enough to keep around as a spare. So from Brazil I made an emergency call to Callaway. The FT-3 has long since been discontinued, so they got a new FT-9 to another player, Leta Lindley, who hadn't left for Rio yet. She was kind enough to bring me my new driver. Unfortunately, I never got comfy with the FT-9 and my tentative swings left me hitting my approach shots from the same places as all the other girls. That shit is tiring! If I had to hit 5-irons into every par-4 like all those short-knockers, I think I'd probably find another line of work.

Arriving in Carlsbad, I went straight to Callaway to get another shaft put into my old FT-3. After the tech guys rebuilt my driver, I spent some time testing it but the feeling still wasn't right. With a heavy heart I concluded that the driver would never be the same and it was time to start searching for a new magic wand, so I headed down the road to TaylorMade. When it comes to equipment, I'm a total slut. I've never signed an exclusive deal with any manufacturer because I want to be able to spread it around to different companies. I had heard a lot of buzz about TaylorMade's new r9 driver and spent a long time testing it. I was definitely impressed and grabbed the driver, a few of the interchangeable shafts that go with it, and a couple of new wedges to potentially use in the future.

My driver hadn't been the only problem during the two tournaments in Asia. I also struggled with distance control of my TaylorMade wedges. The boys in Carlsbad checked them out, and sure enough, the wedges were all screwed up: My 60-degree lob wedge had been bent to 58 degrees, while the lie on my gap wedge was two degrees flatter than usual, which means the toe of the club was pointing downward. (Overpracticing was probably the cause, but the wedges could also have been banged around in transit.) I had suspected they were a little out of whack, but it's too expensive for equipment companies to send their tech guys to Asia, so there was no way of testing the wedges at those tournaments. I was so happy to have a possible explanation for my struggles in Thailand and Singapore. After spending the night in Carlsbad—I had slept only six of the preceding fifty-four hours—I drove to Palm Springs for another scouting mission of Mission Hills Country Club, site of the upcoming Dinah Shore. Using my retooled wedges was as familiar as slipping on an old favorite pair of jeans. They felt better in my hand and looked better to my eye and I hit them beautifully. After the round, Pat Hurst called to invite me to tee it up with her at Papago, so I made the four-hour drive to Phoenix. While in town I also swung by the Ping headquarters to grab a new driver and a new putter. As I said, I like to spread it around.

The rest of the week in Phoenix was spent working on my game and testing out all my new driver and putter possibilities. On Sunday, March 15—six days after I had arrived in the U.S. post-Singapore—I finally flew south of the border. It happened to be my twenty-fifth birthday, and I was happy to be on a plane because I didn't have anything else to do. In the past I've always loved milestone birthdays. Turning sixteen, eighteen, and twenty-one were big because they represented cars, porn, and booze, in that order. Turning twenty-five was a bit of a letdown. The only good thing about it was that I would no longer have to pay underage fees on my rental cars. At the Phoenix airport I had the girl at the rental counter refund me a partial day of charges. Happy birthday to me.

Playing the MasterCard presents certain challenges. Many of the players are paranoid about getting sick, and some go to crazy extremes. Meaghan Francella schlepped a suitcase to Mexico City that was stuffed with Cup o' Noodles, Top Ramen, mac-n-cheese, pretzels, granola bars, peanut butter, Honey Nut Cheerios, and Nutella. That's pretty much all she ate the entire week, though I was happy to help her out by scooping up gobs of Nutella with a few stray pretzels.

The host course, Bosque Real Country Club, is one of the most extreme we play, basically built on the side of a mountain at about eight thousand feet above sea level. Because of the brutal terrain and the elevation and the thick smog it is very, very difficult to walk the course without proper time to acclimate, so the LPGA allows us to ride in carts for the only time all season.

I began my first round on the tenth hole, and waiting to tee off I felt a few extra butterflies because I was using a new putter and a new driver, which are only the two most important clubs in your bag. After much testing and tinkering I had settled on a pair of Pings: the Rapture driver and an Anser putter. To keep from second-guessing the decision, I left behind all the other possibilities in the U.S.

On number ten I pushed my 9-iron approach right of the green and then chipped to six feet. It felt like I made a solid stroke but the par putt was never on line, missing right. On the next hole I had another six-footer to get up and down, and again it rolled over the right edge. My caddie Danny confirmed that I was making a good stroke. This new Ping putter had an unusual neck and suddenly I was having trouble lining up my putts properly. It had felt good in practice, but the pressure of tournament golf does funny things to your mind and body.

I have a tendency to begin a round too jacked up, trying to force birdies, so my dad has always told me to try to play the first three holes in even par. That's what I did, eagling the twelfth hole with a 5-wood from 225 yards out that cozied to within a foot and a half of a flag that was tucked on the left edge of the green. I was actually aiming at the middle of the putting surface but pulled the shot slightly, and as it was in the air I was yelling, "Ohmygawd, ohmygawd, no!" After it finished so close to the hole, Tom Lincicome, the father of my playing partner, Brittany Lincicome, bellowed at me in good fun, "Do you always get so upset with kick-in eagles?"

Unfortunately, that was the only highlight of the day. It seemed like I was missing every putt to the right. It was so demoralizing, and I was furious for having made such a bad decision after tinkering with so many other possible putters. Missing all those putts was wearing me out mentally even before my first nine holes were over. On the par-5 eighteenth hole I hit my layup too far, leaving me an awkward half-wedge approach on a downhill, sidehill lie. A layup on a par-5 should be the easiest shot in the world, and I was so peeved I couldn't properly focus on the next shot, so I got what I deserved: a stubbed wedge into a hazard, which led to a double bogey.

After a lifeless back nine I signed for a 75, fully ten strokes back of the leader, Lorena Ochoa, Mexico's national sweetheart. That was a familiar feeling, as I have been chasing Lorena for most of my golfing life.

It all began when I was fifteen and first getting serious about the game. My dad wanted me to leave our little bubble in Northern California to experience different playing conditions, so we road-tripped to the 1999 Mexican Women's Amateur. Back then Lorena was a little sprite who couldn't have weighed more than eighty pounds, but she already hit the ball a ton. Since I was one of the few Americans in the field, she went out of her way to make me feel welcome. To this day she's one of my best friends and I'm one of her biggest fans. She is the sweetest, kindest, most giving person walking the earth. Any positive word you can use to describe a human being, that would be Lorena Ochoa. She's got that inner light. I think she's been touched by God. Honestly, I'm surprised she hasn't been canonized yet. I'm not exaggerating, she is the greatest thing ever—a cross between Babe Zaharias and Mother Teresa. (Lorena's eponymous foundation underwrites a number of schools in Mexico for disadvantaged kids and funds a program to provide treatment and support for children with cancer in her hometown of Guadalajara.) But Lorena has a mischievous side that few people see. I got my first taste of it at that Mexican Amateur. We had repaired to the clubhouse to celebrate her victory when Lorena and a group of other players brought me a *michelada*. It was so tangy and fizzy and delicious I had two or three more. What I didn't know is that beer is the active ingredient, along with lime juice and salt. So I like to say that when I was fifteen, Lorena Ochoa got me drunk off my ass, and she and I still laugh about it.

We crossed paths again on the Futures Tour in the summer of 2002, right after I turned pro. At the Garden State Futures Golf Classic I earned a spot in the final group of the final round alongside Lorena, who in just a handful of tournaments had established herself as the dominant force on tour. She was already a star in golf circles and even at these Podunk events she attracted a huge following; for our final round together, we were trailed by a nun carrying a Mexican flag. How are you supposed to compete against that?

Lorena and I battled all day and wound up going to a playoff, with both of us shooting 14 under par. After tying the first three holes in sudden death, I didn't care if I won or lost: I just wanted to get out of the brutal July heat. On the twenty-second hole of the day I hit a gorgeous approach shot to a foot. Lorena was thirty feet away and she almost made the putt, leaving it one inch short. I brushed in my birdie for the victory and what remains one of the sweetest moments of my career. Unfortunately, you can't get a good *michelada* in Hackensack, New Jersey.

At the MasterCard I had a chance to catch up with Lorena a little bit. The big news was that a few months earlier, while vacationing in Europe, she had gotten engaged to a dapper older gentleman named Andres Conesa, the CEO of AeroMexico. Telling me about their romance she had this special glow about her. Of course I was thrilled for Lorena, but her engagement is not necessarily good news for the LPGA Tour. Lorena is so family-oriented she has told me in the past that once she has kids she will quit competitive golf cold turkey. I have little doubt that she will retire after the 2012 season. That will give her ten years on tour, the minimum needed to qualify her for the Hall of Fame. She will be thirty-one then and eager to start popping out cute little Mexican babies. Lorena is like a comet passing by—you better enjoy her now, because she will be gone before you know it.

I again began the second round of the MasterCard on the tenth tee and opened with five straight pars, even though I was still fighting my putter. On the fifteenth hole I hit a disgusting 5-wood off the tee, leading to a double bogey. After beating myself up so much during the Asian tournaments I had resolved to try to be more Zenlike on the golf course, but it wasn't happening. I was not enjoying the round at all, and I blame a lot of it on having to ride around in that damn golf cart. I can't play tournament golf in a cart. I always ride when I'm at home in Florida practicing. I like to zip around the course, trying different shots and working on specific parts of my game. When I'm in a cart I'm rarely grinding for a score. The only time I walk is in tournament play, so I associate it with serious golf. Riding in a cart in Mexico City just didn't have a professional feel to me, and I could not summon the proper mentality. On my eleventh hole of the second round I was on the downswing when the shadow of a bug passed over my ball. If I had been locked in mentally it wouldn't have affected my swing, but this time I lost focus for a split second and jerked the shot into a water hazard, leading to another double bogey that ensured I would miss the cut.

After a birdieless 78 I was ready to drown my sorrows, so that night I went out with Dorothy Delasin, who had also missed the cut. We ordered margaritas that came in the biggest glasses I have ever seen. They must have held a gallon each. I had a Tanqueray-and-tonic chaser, and then we went to a swanky Japanese bar and I imbibed a few more, all the while trying to stealthily take a picture of a guy there who had the most astonishing unibrow I had ever seen. After stumbling back to my hotel room I crashed for eleven hours, and when I woke up I was no longer so upset about having missed the cut.

From Mexico City I journeyed directly to Papago for the Phoenix LPGA International. The changes just kept coming. I benched the Ping putter that had betrayed me at the MasterCard and went back to the Yes! Golf putter I'd been using off and on for years. I also decided to ditch the Ping driver and put in play the TaylorMade r9. All the upheaval in my equipment was symptomatic of a larger metamorphosis I was going through. I had been doing a lot of thinking and decided that, in a nutshell, I wanted to become a different person. My big night out with Dorothy in Mexico City was part of me trying to rekindle the many friendships that I had neglected over the preceding two and a half years, when most of my energy was going to my boyfriend. It wasn't until I was out of that relationship that I realized how much of myself I had given up. There were other ways I wanted to transform myself, including physically. On my birthday I resolved that I would dedicate myself to getting into better shape and that I would run a half marathon by the end of the year.

Since my election to the player advisory board I had really been enjoying my new responsibilities, partaking in conference calls with LPGA brass and being part of many conversations and decisions with fellow players and tournament officials. I've always been a little self-conscious about not going to college, and being a player director has shown me I can be comfortable in a leadership position, that I can do something with my life beyond hitting a golf ball. I've started looking into correspondence courses and become determined to work toward a college degree.

Sometimes you seek change and sometimes it is thrust upon you. While I was in Phoenix, I received a stunning voice mail from my longtime agent. She had just been let go from Octagon, one of the biggest agencies in the golf world, and was striking out on her own. She wanted me to join her, but I had other options to consider as I began to be wooed by IMG and others.

Obviously, there was a lot floating around in my head during the week of Phoenix, which probably explains why I went out and finished a middling thirty-ninth. But even though rounds of 72-75-71-73 didn't reflect it, I played very well. It was tough to score because there were some gnarly gusts of wind throughout the week, and the greens at Papago were so bumpy Angela Stanford described them to a reporter as "Plinko"—referencing the game of chance on *The Price Is Right*. I'll never be satisfied finishing in the middle of the pack, but I was encouraged not to have any big blow-up holes—for a change—and that I bombed my new TaylorMade driver, convincing me I had finally found the right big stick to allow me to exploit my power advantage.

Over the season's first five tournaments I had faced so much adversity and uncertainty, but by the end of my four rounds in Phoenix I felt more settled than I had in a long time.

Within minutes of the final putt dropping, I was in the car blazing to Palm Springs for the most glamorous tournament of the year, the Kraft Nabisco Championship. I had a hopeful feeling that it was going to be a good week. I just didn't know how good.

CHAPTER 4

Breakthrough

Upon awakening in Palm Springs, I immediately flashed back to a conversation I'd had the previous evening in the Papago parking lot. (I hadn't had much time for reflection during the harrowing drive from Phoenix, as my rental car was buffeted the whole way by fifty-mile-per-hour winds.) Following my final round at the Phoenix International I had been buttonholed by an LPGA rules official who gave me a long lecture about my on-course comportment. I was told that I needed to improve my attitude and my language and start being a better role model. When the initial shock subsided, I was very grateful for the pep talk. I had been oblivious to the fact that everyone on tour thought I was suffering from a case of permanent PMS. Lying in my hotel bed in Palm Springs, I resolved to go back to being cheerful and positive. I have always tried to be personable with volunteers and fans and my fellow players, but it was clear I had gotten away from that a little bit. Now I was determined to overwhelm them all with kindness.

A funny thing happened when I popped out of bed after making this resolution: I felt like I was floating. My step was lighter and my face muscles weren't tired from being twisted into a frown. I felt energized and instantly happier. The Kraft Nabisco Championship—or Dinah Shore, as the old-timers refer to it, a nod to the former tournament hostess—has always been one of my favorite events on tour, but suddenly I was even more excited about the week. One of my primary goals for 2009 was to win a first major championship, and I couldn't wait to get after it.

The good juju continued when I got to Mission Hills for a practice round. I bumped into a TaylorMade rep who had heard all about my putter woes and he showed me a new model, the Monte Carlo. It was love at first sight. The putter felt great in my hands and the clean styling and black finish looked good to my eye. It went straight into the bag for a practice round, and after a few holes I knew I had finally found the right putter.

The joy I felt with my new wand seeped into the rest of my game and just reinforced my general good cheer. For the first round, I went off the tenth tee and began with five straight pars. There was none of my usual restlessness about making birdies. I was content to just keep hitting solid shots. On the fifteenth hole, a twelve-footer for birdie dropped in and I was like, OMMFG, I just made a putt! It seemed like it had been months since the last time that had happened. On the seventeenth, a tricky little 163-yard par-3, I hit a scandalous 7-iron that was well right of my intended line, but it took a good hop on the edge of the green and then funneled off a big swale on the putting surface to within six feet of the cup. My caddie Danny and

I just looked at each other, eyebrows arched. I had been suffering through bad luck all season, and normally that ball would
have kicked the other way and buried under the lip of a bunker
next to a squirrel's acorn. Taking advantage of the good for-
tune, I brushed in the birdie putt to go to two under par.

On the par-5 eighteenth hole, the tees were up and a good
drive left me with 230 yards to the hole, 210 to clear the water
hazard fronting the green. Ordinarily I would have gone for
the green without a second thought, but this time I just wasn't
feeling it. I didn't want to do anything reckless after such a
great break on seventeen. So I laid up and then stuck my wedge
to twelve feet. Not to be immodest, but the galleries at the
Dinah have loved me ever since I finished eighth there during
my second year on tour. The grandstand at eighteen is always
packed and boisterous, and when I buried that birdie putt the
roar was deafening.

So I was three under making the turn. I knew that put me
among the leaders, but I felt strangely relaxed. I was determined not to stress about my score and just continue to enjoy
the walk. The second hole at Mission Hills is a long, straight
par-5, and I always try to reach it in two, though I rarely do,
usually leaving an awkward half-wedge third shot from too
close to the green. This time my drive found a fairway bunker,
forcing me to lay up. An adroit second shot left ninety-six yards
for my approach shot, the perfect number for my 56-degree
wedge. I stuffed it to eight feet and made my fourth birdie of
the day. A bogey at five was offset by another bird at seven, and
I just kept floating along. However, a three-putt on the eighth
hole put my new carefree attitude to the test. Bogeys are a fact
of life, but for some reason a three-putt infuriates me way more

than, say, a bogey out of a bunker, because it feels like more of an unforced error. I was still pretty steamed on the tee of the par-5 ninth and didn't do a good job of getting refocused, leading to a badly hooked drive. My ball was screaming toward a grove of trees about 140 yards off the tee, but we never saw where it landed. A big search ensued, and the whole time I had the sickening feeling that my ball would be lost and my whole round was going to be ruined. But Nate Hair, the husband of my playing partner Wendy Ward, miraculously found the ball. It was thirty yards shorter and much farther left than we had thought, just inside an out-of-bounds line I never knew existed. Instead of being upset by how horrid the drive was I was elated just to have located my ball. I played a gutsy recovery, a low, slinging 8-iron through a half dozen trees. That still left me 242 yards to the hole, and my ensuing 3-wood came up just short. An awesome flop over a bunker left me five feet from the hole, and I poured in the putt for a par that felt like an eagle. That capped a 69 that left me tied for sixth place, just three strokes off Brittany Lincicome's lead.

Walking out of the scorer's tent, Wendy Ward, one of the tour's real sweethearts, told me, "That was a great round of golf. You faced adversity and overcame it. I'm really proud of you."

I immediately waded into the autograph tent and happily signed for about a hundred fans, thanking them profusely for having stood in line. When one guy said he had gotten my autograph years earlier, I gave him a crushing hug and was like, "Ohmygod, it's so amazing to see you again!" Never mind that I had no recollection of having ever laid eyes on him.

Nothing like a shiny round of 69 to help with a new attitude adjustment.

Besides the excellent course and big purse and network telecast, one of the reasons the Dinah feels like a major championship is that the crowds are among the largest we see all season. What's cool about the tournament is that anyone can come and feel welcome. It's no secret that the weekend of the Dinah, the Palm Springs area also hosts the so-called lesbian spring break, which annually attracts twenty-five thousand or so women from all over the country who congregate for a few days of fun and sun. Some of these gals are golf fans, and they definitely add a different dimension to the Dinah's gallery, although nobody's getting it on in a tree à la *Happy Gilmore*. Still, all the openness spotlights a thorny issue for the tour. The LPGA's unofficial public stance about its members' sexual orientation has always been don't ask, don't tell, which is why only two players have ever come out publicly—and they waited until the ends of their careers to do it. Because there has never been an honest, open discussion about lesbianism on tour, it has become a source of fascination among many golf fans— and especially male reporters—who have only heard various rumors and innuendo.

Contrary to what many people think, we are not the Lesbians Playing Golf Association. By my count, there are no more than two dozen gay women playing the tour right now. Considering there are 230 active members, you're only talking about 10 percent of the players, which from everything I've read is in line with the population as a whole.

I understand that, thanks to Howard Stern and Internet porn, many guys are keenly interested in girl-on-girl action, but to every player I know the issue is just not that big a deal. There are no superfreaky homophobes out here or militant man haters or any other extremists. At most, a player's sexuality may be an occasional practice-round conversation piece:

"Hey, did you hear so-and-so likes girls?"

"Really? Huh. So, did you hit an eight-iron or a nine?"

The only downside I can see is that the gay players who want to keep their private lives private may not let reporters, and by extension the public, get to know them, and that can be a big loss to the tour. The greatest couple I've ever known, of any orientation, is a pair of LPGA players. They are so sweet and loving with each other, and everyone I know admires what they have and we all wish we could be as happy in our own romantic lives. Both of these players have enjoyed very successful careers. In this age of Ellen DeGeneres and Rachel Maddow, it's easy to say they should've come out a long time ago; they would be terrific role models to a lot of people, and no doubt there would have been a lot of media interest any time they were paired together or sharing the same leaderboard. But these women have always been very protective about their relationship. To them, missing out on endorsement deals and magazine features is a small price to pay for privacy.

I know not everyone shares my left-leaning California sensibilities, but a week at the Dinah might change a few minds. Seeing so many happy golf fans together—gay and straight—is an annual reminder to live and let live.

*   *   *   *

At the start of the second round I had the same lighthearted, carefree feeling as the day before, and I played the front nine in an effortless 32, making four birdies against no bogeys. Walking to the tenth tee I saw a scoreboard and was pleasantly surprised to discover that I was leading the tournament, at −7. Any other week of my life I probably would have had a mini freak-out and started walking faster, talking faster, and swinging faster. This time I just said to myself, twenty-seven holes doesn't make a tournament, so just keep doing what you're doing. It didn't happen.

I made a mess of the tenth hole and was left with a fifty-footer for par. I missed the putt by an inch and was so satisfied with the effort the bogey didn't bother me. On thirteen I drove it into the right rough, slashed a 7-iron short of the green, and failed to get up and down. It was a routine bogey and I accepted it with a good attitude. Now, bogeying the fourteenth, that was infuriating. I hit a perfect drive and had only a wedge left, but my second shot missed the green. To make matters worse, I then played a horrible chip, leaving it six feet short, and then blew the putt. I was raging as I walked off the green but my caddie Danny gave me a nice little pep talk that settled me down a bit. I parred the next two holes, which wasn't easy, as the wind was beginning to howl. On the par-3 seventeenth hole I smashed a low 6-iron to the center of the green and again my ball took the slope perfectly, inching toward the hole. On the tee box I could hear clapping, then murmuring, then a roar that was getting progressively louder. I knew that meant my ball was inching closer and closer to the hole, and arriving at the green I was delighted to discover I had only six feet left for birdie. I made the putt for my first bird of the back nine, getting me back to −5.

On the eighteenth hole I lost my tee shot to the right but got another lucky break as my ball doinked a palm tree and ricocheted into the fairway. With a laugh I said to my caddie, "Dude, this week rocks." I ripped a 3-wood through the wind and played a lovely, low, punched pitching wedge to six feet, draining the putt for another birdie. My 69 had tied me for the clubhouse lead with Kristy McPherson, and with a crazy windstorm blowing through the Coachella Valley, it didn't seem likely any of the players going off in the afternoon would be able to stay with us.

After signing my scorecard I was led to the press room for a group interview, an event my friends in the media delicately call the gangbang. Some players consider press conferences to be the equivalent of being fed to vultures, but I've always loved the attention and the repartee with the reporters. It had been almost a year since the last time I was in the press room, and it was nice to see some familiar faces and old friends. The general reaction among the scribes was, Where the hell have you been? I talked about my new attitude and my new putter, and by the time I was done with the interviews I had dozens of text messages from friends, family, and fellow players. I was spooning up all of the fawning but at the same time trying hard to remain mellow. I knew there were still two long, tough rounds ahead.

All the buzz on Saturday morning was about the fifty-mile-per-hour gusts that had made the afternoon of the second round a brutal test of the players' survival skills. I was glad to have missed most of the gales but also felt a little guilty, like maybe I hadn't truly earned my share of the lead. I would be playing in the final twosome with my coleader, McPherson, and that definitely led to a few butterflies. It had been a long time since my last cameo in a final pairing, and it had never happened at a major. Prior to teeing off I tried to lose myself in my routine, hoping it would steady my nerves.

Before every tournament round I have the same ninety-minute ritual. I start by putting for fifteen minutes and then chipping for five. The next forty minutes are spent on the range, hitting every club in my bag. I've always had this horrible fear that if I don't test each stick ahead of time and reestablish a personal connection I won't know how to hit it out on the course. The order is always the same, although it has more to do with habit and superstition than anything scientific: driver, pitching wedge, 8-, 6-, 4-, 5-, 7-, and 9-irons, followed by 5-wood and then 3-wood. Then I go through my three wedges—52-degree gap, 56-degree sandy, 60-degree lob—and end with at least five swings with my drivers. I won't leave the range until I've hit at least two perfect drives in a row. Another twenty minutes are spent putting and chipping—I'll spend more time on whichever discipline feels like it needs a little extra attention—and then I matriculate to the tee box, careful not to arrive more than five minutes early because just standing there I get more and more antsy.

When the third round of the Dinah began I was swinging at it great, and I opened with six straight pars. The solid start helped me to relax a little, but playing in the final group is just a strange feeling. There's more reporters and cameramen following you and jockeying for space inside the ropes, which always leads to a certain amount of commotion with the persnickety marshals. Fans are clearing out of the grandstands before you finish putting out, and the maintenance crew is hot on your heels, going to work on each hole as soon as you're finished with it. Maintaining your focus is definitely a challenge.

I made my only mistake of the front nine on number seven, leaving my approach short of the green and missing a six-footer for par. I turned in one-over 37 but was still feeling pretty patient, confident that I was still in the thick of the tournament. The early part of the back nine was when it all began to slip away. Kristy birdied ten, eleven, and twelve and I started feeling antsy to keep up but couldn't convert any in a series of good birdie opportunities. It didn't help that from the crowd noise and an occasional peek at the scoreboard I could tell that Brittany Lincicome and Cristie Kerr were both making a bunch of birdies. The anxiety I was feeling came out on the fifteenth hole. I drove it in the rough but still decided to play a very aggressive shot to a pin tucked into a tiny front-left corner of the green. This was a classic sucker pin, because only a sucker would be foolish enough to aim for it given the fraught location. I flew my approach too far, leaving an impossible downhill forty-five-footer with about five feet of break. Naturally I three-putted, costing me another bogey.

With three holes to go I had not yet made a birdie. Now the tournament became almost secondary as I became determined to make at least one birdie and avoid the dreaded shutout. After pars on sixteen and seventeen, the closing hole was my last shot. I wanted so badly to bust a long drive that I swung too hard and yanked my shot way left. All of my good luck must have been used up over the first two days, because my ball hit a palm tree and bounced dead left, into the lake. All the adrenaline instantly drained out of my body. Not only was I not going to make birdie, it was going to be a struggle just to save par. After taking a penalty drop I managed to hit two credible shots, leaving a fifteen-foot putt to save par. Didn't happen. I gunned it by the hole and now faced five feet for bogey. I was proud of myself for having the wherewithal to make the comebacker, closing the books on a birdieless 75. At −3 I was now in sixth place, five back of Kristy McPherson. Of course I was disappointed, but I also felt like I still had a chance to win going into the final round. Plenty of players have made up five strokes on a Sunday, and the Dinah has a long history of surprise endings.

After the round, I spent twenty minutes in the autograph tent. I didn't really want to go—I mean, who would?—but I smiled my way through it, and the good vibes from the fans helped cheer me up a bit. After I putted out on eighteen I had looked at the scoreboard and calculated that my final-round playing partner would be Meaghan Francella, which I was excited about because she's a good friend who's a lot of fun on the course. But en route to the driving range I received some different news from a tournament official. For the final round we would be playing threesomes, meaning I was to be paired with Jimin Kang and Lindsey Wright. Hearing that, my stomach dropped. I like both players a lot—that wasn't the issue. The very big problem was that Lindsey's caddie was Mark Britton, which meant I was going to have to spend one of the most important rounds of my life alongside my ex-boyfriend.

On Sunday I was deep into my preround routine when my cell phone bleated from inside my golf bag. Uncharacteristically,

I had forgotten to turn the phone off, and I decided to check who was calling. It was Dad, ringing from Korea, where it was about one A.M. He never calls me before a round, so I wondered what was bothering him. "Be aggressive today," he barked. "Focus hard. Make birdie." I had never heard so much intensity in his voice. I knew he wasn't going to sleep a wink.

My dad's pep talk helped take my mind off the impending awkwardness with Mark. I was dreading our first interaction, but it turned out not to be a big deal. We had been pointedly ignoring each other for a while on the expansive practice green when we suddenly wound up standing right next to each other. I just tapped him on the shoulder and was like, Have a great day, buddy. The whole situation had the potential to be pathetic and high schooly, but I was determined to rise above it. I had a job to do and this tournament meant way too much to me to let it be ruined by my female emotions. I expend so much energy competing, there was no way I'd survive the round if I got caught up trying to somehow stick it to my ex-boyfriend. I just saw the pairing as yet another challenge, the ultimate test of my new and improved attitude.

With so much to play for I came out flying, rolling in a twenty-five-foot birdie putt on the first hole.

Mark's response: "Nice putt."

My reply: "Thanks."

On the par-3 third hole I smoked a 7-iron from 169 yards to within five feet of the hole and then poured in the putt for another birdie. Kristy McPherson had bogeyed the second hole, and just like that I had picked up three shots on her, though Cristie Kerr had pushed the lead to −9 with birdies on the second and fourth holes. The pins were in tough spots on Sunday and the wind was swirling, so I was happy to par the next five holes. On the tee of the par-5 ninth hole I was in my downswing when a photographer started snapping pictures. To me it was as loud and shocking as gunfire and I blew my drive way right. The other players and caddies in the group were furious and pointed out the offending snapper to a rules official, who was last seen chasing down the photographer. I was pretty frazzled by the whole thing and spent the rest of the hole struggling to regain my composure. I punched out of the trees and then hit what felt like a perfect approach shot, but it landed about three feet short and spun back fifteen yards in front of the green. I was still out of my rhythm, playing a little too quickly, and wound up flubbing the ensuing pitch, which led to a very disappointing bogey. Meanwhile, the girls behind me in the final pairing were on a birdie binge. When Kristy and Brittany both birdied the ninth hole they were at −8, one back of Kerr. Spinning my wheels at −4, I needed to play the best nine holes of my life to have a chance.

My ball striking was up to the challenge but I couldn't get the putts to drop. Four birdie tries on the back nine should've gone in but didn't, including a five-footer on number fifteen and a fifteen-footer on sixteen. I wound up shooting 72, which left me in seventh place, ultimately six strokes back of Brittany Lincicome, who made a spectacular eagle on the final hole to win by one.

After I had putted out on eighteen, Mark and I shared a very businesslike hug. It was the closure I needed, and it felt like something ended right there. In a lot of ways the Dinah was a new beginning for me. Sure, I would have liked to have played a little better over the final two rounds, but I took so many positives out of the week. I proved to myself that my game is good enough to win a major. More important, I had so much fun every day, even with the myriad challenges. I didn't leave Palm Springs with a trophy but I still counted the week as a victory because I rediscovered who I am, and how good I can be.

CHAPTER 5

Roots

Shortly before the season began, one of the LPGA's marquee tournaments, the Ginn Tribute, vanished from the
schedule, owing to the economic woes of the title sponsor, a
large-scale real estate development company. The Tribute was
to have been played right after the Kraft Nabisco, so its disap-
pearance meant there was only one tournament in the ensuing
four weeks. That event, the Corona Championship, is played
on a course I don't exactly love, so I decided to skip it and take a
long holiday in Korea to enjoy some relaxing time with my parents and extended family. At least that was the plan.

Immediately after the final round of the Kraft, my mom and
I hauled ass to L.A. to catch our flight. There wasn't even time
for me to shower, but I didn't really mind because top-ten
sweat has a nice smell, like crisp dollar bills. My dad had already been over in Korea for a while and had hatched a plan
for me to have my quarter-century tune-up during my visit.
Dad is friendly with many doctors and hospital administrators,

so shortly after my arrival in Seoul I was put through a battery
of tests on state-of-the-art equipment, all for free. This was not
really about my performance as an athlete—the goal was not
to turn me into the Russian guy from *Rocky IV*—but just to
make sure that I'm healthy and normal, or as normal as I can
be. American doctors' offices smell like formaldehyde, which
makes me gag, and so I have always avoided these kinds of
checkups. But I don't mind being in the medical buildings in
Korea because they miraculously smell like Oreos. After being
poked and prodded and measured and examined and CT-
scanned for the better part of three days the verdict came back
that my death is not imminent. So I have that going for me.
Which is nice.

After five days in Korea I was just beginning to get adjusted
to the local time, but then I had to abruptly fly back to the U.S.
When the trip to Seoul was booked I had been confused about
the dates of an LPGA board meeting and the confab turned out
to be two weeks earlier than I thought. As a newbie player director I didn't feel right skipping the meeting, so I caught a
flight to L.A., endured a seven-hour layover, red-eyed to Orlando, and then drove to the LPGA headquarters in Daytona
Beach, arriving just a couple hours before the board meetings
began. It was a kamikaze mission, obviously, but my peers
elected me to do a job and I'm determined to do it to the best
of my ability. As a member of the governance committee, much
of my time in Daytona was spent discussing ways to modernize
the LPGA constitution, which has barely been touched since
1976. (There are places where it still states that official correspondence must be received via certified mail. This always
makes me laugh—it might as well say carrier pigeon, as these

days everything is done via e-mail and text message.) After the meeting, the player directors and LPGA brass gathered for a fun dinner at which the conversation and wine flowed freely. The next day I returned to Korea, arriving there about ninety hours after my departure.

For my second stint in Seoul, my parents and I stayed in neighboring rooms at a hotel in the fashionable Apgujeong district. My mom and I really enjoyed the bonding time. In 2008, when I was still with Boyfriend, she came to only one tournament all season. So far in '09 she had already been to two events and now we had all this time together in Seoul, where we shopped, went to the spa, got mani-pedis, watched endless hours of Discovery Channel DVDs, and just talked and talked. We've always had an interesting relationship. She is the stereotypical Korean mom: quiet, reserved, sweet, and she always thinks before she speaks. Basically she's my polar opposite, and I'm sure she has been more than a little mortified by me through the years. But as I've gotten older I think Mom understands me better and I know I appreciate her more. I've actually become very protective of her. When she's with me at tournaments I'm always hyperaware of where she is and what she's doing and forever fretting that some misfortune will befall her. It's not easy raising parents.

I had schlepped my golf clubs to Korea but never used them, unless you count a few lazy swings in my hotel room. Instead I spent the time trying to better myself in other ways. Working toward one of my long-standing goals, I took a laborious online course covering all the book work to get certified for scuba, and with some diligent studying I aced all of the tests. I also did a lot of thinking about how I can have an impact beyond golf. Many players on tour are involved with extremely worthy causes. To cite just a few examples, Morgan Pressel, Val Skinner, and Cristie Kerr raise money for breast-cancer research, Paula Creamer is a spokesperson for the Arnold Palmer Hospital for Children in Orlando, and, through her eponymous foundation, Lorena Ochoa has numerous initiatives to better the lives of children in Mexico. I respect all of these efforts so much, but I can't take on similar causes because I don't really like people. I don't have much faith in society or humanity. There are a lot of individuals I consider dear friends, but collectively humans are so destructive and wasteful. So after a lot of rumination I resolved to be a voice for those things that can't speak for themselves—animals, rain forests, oceans. Conservation and sustainability are going to be my focus, and from Korea I began brainstorming on how to reduce my carbon footprint and peppering my agents and fellow players and LPGA officials with ideas on the best ways for me to personally save the planet.

I also resolved to get in better physical condition. I visited a nutritionist to advise me on a healthier diet, and he also prescribed the magic pill Orlistat to help my body burn fat more effectively. These meds are identical to the popular diet pill Alli that's sold in the U.S., but double the dose—120 milligrams—because Koreans don't do anything halfway. (And, yes, I did check with the LPGA to make sure Orlistat is not a banned substance under our performance-enhancing-drug policy.) Not only do these pills burn fat, but they force you to eat much better because of the two scariest words in the English language: *anal leakage.* Turns out that if you consume too much fatty food while taking Orlistat your body can't process it properly and a lot of yucky stuff just sort of leaks out. That put the fear of God into me, so during my three weeks in Korea I cut out virtually all fatty foods. I also abstained from carbs and didn't allow myself to consume anything with sugar, not even fruit juice. The results were immediate: I dropped twelve pounds, though that put me less than a third of the way toward my eventual goal.

This is the second time that being in Korea has helped me to get into better shape. The first occasion was the winter following my third year on tour. To that point I had teed it up in ninety-five of the ninety-six tournaments for which I was eligible. Worn out from the grind, I vowed in December 2005 to drastically improve my fitness. I was also spurred by my dad, who, with typical delicacy, had declared, "You too fat. You need lose forty pound to make you better golfer."

So I moved in with family in Korea and began to work my ass off (literally). The alarm went off every day at five A.M. for a five-mile run, and this was followed by two hours in the gym doing weight training and various exotic forms of torture. Then I would go for long sessions of deep-tissue massages and acupuncture. They focused on the juicy areas where fat is stored, and it was excruciating. These little old ladies would say, "Ah, look, poison is leaking out of body!" I would be thinking, *No, bitch, I'm crying because you're hurting me!*

I also endured a fun-free diet heavy on rice and fish and kimchi. I can't say I enjoyed my winter over there but the desired forty pounds were shed, and at the start of the 2006 season I was suddenly the LPGA's It Girl. Remember the first day of school in junior high when there was always a classmate who over the summer had grown boobs, got her braces

off, and had a new haircut and suddenly everyone was notic-
ing her for the first time? I used to hate that girl, and now I
was her. A lot more media attention and autograph requests
came my way, and even fellow players who had ignored me in
the past seemed to be a lot nicer. It's kind of sad, really, that
people treated me so differently just because I had lost some
weight, but I guess that's the way it is in a culture obsessed
with appearance.

Slowly, inevitably, I became less disciplined in my jogging
and diet, and by the start of the 2009 season I was fat and lazy
again. Getting fit will surely help my stamina on the golf
course and no doubt make me feel better about myself. Yes,
I'm a professional athlete, but I suffer from all the same inse-
curities as any other woman, and it's magnified by having so
many eyeballs on me during a tournament. There have been
many days when I don't like my hair or makeup or the way my
clothes fit, and it's hard to play well when you're unhappy
with how you look.

I'm certainly not alone in fighting the body-image battles.
Even players who I think are hot spend a lot of time worrying
about their appearance. I know this because it's always one of
the primary topics in the locker room. For a long time I was
convinced that one of the really tall, pretty girls on tour had an
eating disorder. She was unnaturally skinny and her teeth had
that yellow look that comes from the acid wearing away the
enamel when you are always throwing up your meals. I've
heard this player sought out treatment, and in the last year or
so she's looked a lot healthier.

It's fine if losing a bit of weight gets me noticed more, but
lately boys are the last thing on my mind. After the final-round

drama at the Dinah Shore it felt like I was finally over the breakup with Mark, but I still wasn't ready to start dating again. The whole time in Korea I didn't have a single naughty thought about the opposite sex, probably the longest I've gone since puberty.

I'm not sure what it is about being in Korea that inspires self-improvement. It must be something cultural—everyone over there works so hard and takes such pride in their craft, whether it's a shoe shiner or manicurist or bellhop. I wish American golf fans and sportswriters could spend some time in Korea to get a better understanding of the country that continues to change the face of the LPGA. There are so many misconceptions and misunderstandings, and it's been that way for far too long. By the time I reached the LPGA Tour, the stereotype of the emotionless Korean golfer with an overbearing father was already an enduring cliché. Like pretty much all things concerning Korean golf, it can be traced to Se Ri Pak. When she won the 1998 U.S. Women's Open and LPGA Championship as a steely twenty-year-old rookie, she sparked a golf boom in her homeland that is still being felt. During Pak's rookie year she was one of only two Koreans on tour. Now there are four dozen, and this immigration is going to continue inexorably given the infrastructure in Korea: a vast number of golf academies and junior programs and playing opportunities on the KLPGA. Virtually every story about Pak's breakthrough focused on her overzealous father, Joon Chul, who famously made Se Ri spend a night alone in a graveyard when she was a teenager because he thought it would make her tougher mentally. He also bragged about never allowing Se Ri to use the elevator in their apartment building so as to strengthen her legs, which doesn't sound like a big deal but for the fact that they lived on the fifteenth floor.

The next great player to come out of Korea, Mi Hyun Kim, had her own tale of woe: Her dad vowed not to let her get married until she won a major championship. Super Peanut, as we all call Mi Hyun because she's only five foot one, won eight LPGA events from 1999 to 2007 but could never break through in the majors, and no wonder, given the pressure. She was finally allowed to get married in December 2008, when she was pushing thirty-two, her dad having had a change of heart when Peanut was courted by Won Hee Lee, a national hero in Korea for having won a gold medal in judo at the 2004 Athens Olympics. (Se Ri caught the bouquet at the wedding, though she remains unmarried, like the vast majority of her countrywomen on tour.)

As more Koreans arrived every year on the LPGA, the culture clash began to produce some strained feelings. Jan Stephenson, the veteran from Australia, created a media firestorm in 2003 when she was quoted as saying, "The Asians are killing our tour. Absolutely killing it [because of] their lack of emotion, their refusal to speak English . . ." Since virtually every Asian on the LPGA was in fact Korean, it was quite clear whom Stephenson was talking about.

In the aftermath of those imprudent remarks, there were more efforts by the tour and individual players to foster communication and cultural understanding. There was some halting progress on those fronts, but in the summer of 2008 another media controversy raged when word leaked out that the LPGA was on the verge of enacting a policy mandating that all players—Korean or not—be conversant in English, with suspensions to be doled out for those who failed the tour's oral exams. The LPGA is always dying for mainstream exposure, but charges of xenophobia are not the reason we want to land on A1 of the *New York Times*. In defending the LPGA's thinking, commissioner Carolyn Bivens said, "The language is part of the control the parents have over their young daughters. If they don't even know survival English, they're totally dependent on the dad."

Because of the public outcry the LPGA eventually modified its stance, making fluency an aspirational goal but not mandatory while also dropping the threat of punitive suspensions. No doubt the whole thing could have been handled more delicately, but I don't think it's outrageous to ask that the players on tour be able to speak some English. The LPGA is based in the U.S. and the majority of our tournaments are still conducted in America. We're in the entertainment business, and it's important to be able to communicate with our fans and the media. It's also vital to be able to properly understand tournament and rules officials, which is why at the Japan LPGA Qualifying tournament players who don't speak the language are mandated to pay for a translator (at upward of five hundred dollars a day). Many of the Korean players and parents who were most outraged by the LPGA's proposed policy were unable to convey their thoughts to American reporters and thus couldn't be part of the public dialogue, which in a weird way validated the LPGA's whole point.

English remains a defining factor for the Koreans on tour. I'd estimate that only 10 percent of them are comfortable enough with their English to interact with all of the other players. The other 90 percent of Koreans break down into two distinct groups. About half of them lead very solitary lives. They are usually the youngest girls—around twenty years old or even younger, having left school in their midteens to turn pro—and they travel with one or both parents. If they're not on the golf course they are on the range or putting green or in their hotel room resting so they can practice even more the next day. The other Koreans move in small, insular groups of four or five or six girls, and they're as self-contained and dependent upon each other as a bobsled team. They play practice rounds together, hit balls next to each other, and eat every meal together. Some of the cliques even have nicknames. One is the self-styled GMG, for Golf Maniac Girls. Some of these little gaggles are known to enjoy a series of wagers at every tournament, paying each other up to a hundred dollars per birdie and assigning cash values to statistics like fewest number of putts per round.

Naturally, the Koreans speak their native tongue when they are together, and I can understand why non-Koreans might hesitate to try to insinuate themselves. I've had to work hard to develop friendships with many of the Koreans because they've never known quite what to make of me. I look like them—well, I do have the same dark hair, slanted eyes, and cute button nose—but I definitely don't sound like them or act like them or dress like them. Spending just a little time among the tour's many Koreans makes it very obvious that this group is not nearly as monolithic and homogenous as people think. Angela Park was born in Brazil; she is a committed Christian who is also well-known for shaking her thing on the dance floor. Jane Park is a brainy California girl with a UCLA education, and she's as apple-pie American as any of the blonde-haired, blue-eyed chicks on tour. She also has an edgy, sexy side that has melted many hearts. Grace Park projects an image of beauty and glamour, but she has an R-rated sense of humor and is one of the LPGA's original divas, having single-handedly introduced Prada and Gucci to the tour. The fans and reporters who grouse, "Oh, those Koreans are all the same" are just too lazy or narrowminded to make the effort to get to know the individuals.

It also bugs me that the Koreans are collectively demonized as "robotic" because they spend so much time trying to improve as players. This is America—don't we celebrate hard work and initiative? The Korean work ethic is certainly respected by the other players. At the 2009 Kraft Nabisco, where five of the top seven finishers were from the U.S., Texas's own Angela Stanford was quoted as saying, "The negativity you sometimes hear about the Asian players is so sad, because by working so hard they have made everybody better. They've forced all of the rest of us to keep up with them, and you're seeing the results now."

No doubt there are still some over-the-top Korean fathers who exploit their daughters' cultural deference by pushing them too hard. There is an infamous story from a couple years ago when one of the overzealous dads was caddying for his girl in a practice round at the Dinah Shore. Unhappy with her play, he simply dropped the bag and walked off the course, forcing her to enlist a gallery member to carry her clubs. But there are plenty of American girls with big, round eyes whose parents are a little too pushy or claustrophobic and I've seen their ranks increase in recent years as the money has gotten bigger and bigger. Oh, and here's one thing that every player is very aware of but most fans don't know: The LPGA's biggest revenue stream is from Korean TV networks paying for the rights to broad-cast our tournaments in Korea. So the next time someone grouses that the Koreans are killing the LPGA, I hope it will be pointed out that, in this economy, it is Korean money that is keeping the tour afloat.

I returned from my long sojourn to Seoul on April 28, sleeping in my own bed at home in Orlando for the first time in two and a half months, dating all the way back to before the season be-gan. After two days of fighting jet lag and doing laundry and catching up with friends, I traveled to Williamsburg, Virginia, for one of the best tournaments of the year, the Michelob Ultra Open. I was dying to get my game back in shape, but my first day and a half at the tournament was spent sitting on my butt at a mandatory players' summit chock full of guest speakers like Billie Jean King and various symposiums on how we can better connect with fans and sponsors. It was very uplifting stuff, and I was honored to be asked by the LPGA president, Michelle Ellis, to give a rah-rah speech as part of the closing festivities. But as the first round began I still felt pretty rusty, and it didn't help that I was putting extra pressure on myself to play well be-cause the year before I had finished as runner-up to Annika Sorenstam. I drove the ball wildly throughout the round and could never get the speed of the greens right, and when I added up all the bogeys my score was an embarrassing 79. This was not exactly the triumphant return to the tour I had been envisioning.

Over the first two rounds I was in the late-early wave, mean-ing my afternoon tee time on Thursday would be followed by a

morning time the following day. Late-early sucks because by
the time you finish your first round you already feel rushed to
get some rest for the next day. So for sheer convenience my
mom and I decided to go to a nearby Ruby Tuesday's for dinner. I had a spinach salad and steak-and-shrimp combo. All the
food looked and tasted fine, but as I was going to bed I was hit
by severe stomach cramps, the first sign of food poisoning.
Thus began the worst night of my life.

I spent the next eight hours in the bathroom, during which it
was coming out of both ends. My mom and I were sharing a
two-bedroom condo, and I was crying and moaning so loud
she said it sounded like I was giving birth. The only sleep I got
was when I passed out on the floor a couple of times. I was still
feeling utterly miserable when I realized that light was peeking
in through the curtains, meaning my eight forty A.M. tee time
was approaching. Despite my misery I was still determined to
play. I've withdrawn from only one tournament in my career
and pride myself on being a gamer. Especially coming on the
heels of the summit, I felt like I owed it to the tour and the tournament to be out there. What if a whole family of Christina
Kim fans was coming to cheer for me and I let them down? Or
what if I happened to be the favorite player of an important executive at a big corporation that was a potential new tournament sponsor? I'm an athlete and sometimes you gotta play
hurt. I strapped on a pair of dark sunglasses and headed to the
course.

Arriving at the practice putting green I must have looked
like death warmed over considering the looks I was getting
and everyone asking me variants of "What the hell is wrong with
you?" I was so dizzy and exhausted, my first practice putt was a

six-footer that was off line by about three feet. Embarrassed, I furtively looked around to see if anybody was watching. After running to the ladies' room due to a few aftershocks, it was time to head to the driving range to warm up. The range at the Kingsmill Resort is a long way from the clubhouse, and suddenly I had a horrifying thought. I asked my caddie if there was a bathroom at the range and he grimly shook his head no. That clinched it, I was withdrawing. I didn't want to make *SportsCenter* for soiling myself on the practice tee.

I was so sad and delirious and emotionally exhausted I spent the next forty-five minutes crying on the shoulders of the tournament director and various LPGA officials. Of course everyone was very understanding. By the time I pulled myself together it was a few minutes before eight forty so I wandered down to the first tee to give my playing partners a send-off. I also wanted to find the volunteers in our group and express my regrets for letting them down. The scorekeeper and standard-bearer each got a hug and an autographed golf ball. They were both middle-aged ex-military guys and they were so sweet and kind I got teary eyed talking to them. The grandstand was very close to the tee box, so eventually the fans figured out what was going on. When I started to walk away they gave me a big ovation, which only made my eyes water even more.

I spent the next twenty-four hours in bed being tended to by my mom, a Korean Florence Nightingale. I didn't eat a thing, but by the next morning I felt well enough to lie on the backseat while Mom drove us seven hours to Clifton, New Jersey, site of the following week's Sybase Classic. My dad had been so concerned—first by my 79 and then by the food poisoning—he flew in from Orlando, so we picked him up at the airport. That evening my appetite finally returned a little bit so I told my parents to find a Korean restaurant. We might have been in the wilds of New Jersey, but I needed something that tasted like home.

CHAPTER 6

Searching

The only good thing about the food-poisoning episode was that exorcising the demonic food baby helped me drop another dress size. At the start of the year I was barely squeezing into a 12. By the week after Williamsburg I was down to a 9, hoping to get to a 4, willing to settle for a perfect size 6.

I was definitely still weakened during the practice rounds of the Sybase Classic. By the start of the first round, my stamina was pretty close to 100 percent. The only problem was that subsisting heavily on liquids for nearly a week had left my extremities feeling bloated and puffy, especially my fingers, which were like big sausages. No surprise, then, that I struggled with my scoring touch throughout an opening 74 at Upper Montclair Country Club. The club felt a lot more comfortable in my hands for the second round and I got off to a pretty hot start, making a fifteen-footer for eagle on the 470-yard par-5 fifth hole. The shot that set it up was a 5-wood from two hundred yards out. It was hit terribly thin and carried the water by only a few paces. My dad and a few friends were near the green, and as my ball cozied up to the flag they went crazy, hooting and hollering. I had to laugh because they had no idea how shitty the strike was and I certainly wasn't going to tell them. I played pretty solid golf the rest of the way, posting a 70 that allowed me to make the cut with ease. Given my lifelessness at the start of the week, I thought that was a nice little accomplishment.

Trying to relocate my game was challenging enough, but I had a very busy week off the course, too. The tournament was run by Octagon, my management company. After my long-time agent had been fired a couple of months earlier I explored a few different options for representation but ultimately decided to stick with Octagon, where a pair of senior agents would handle my affairs. Over two dinners at the Sybase I met with a handful of Octagon people and laid out my various concerns, along with my hopes and dreams. At that point in the season I was making exactly $0.00 through endorsements. I was fully aware of the tough economic climate and the fact that my appeal is, shall we say, nontraditional, but still. There are broads on tour who have never won a thing with shirts covered by corporate logos. I encouraged the Octagon suits to try to find companies offering products that dovetailed with my burgeoning environmentalism. Since my awakening in Korea, I had been doing a lot of reading about the global shortage of clean water. As a result I had begun taking shorter showers and lugging around a little purifier to use on the tap water in my hotel rooms, thus sparing the planet an endless trail of empty plastic bottles. Within days of our dinners, my peeps at Octagon had contacted PUR water and an endorsement deal was in the works.

I was also busy during the week of the Sybase catering to a visitor named Anthony (pronounced with a silent *h*, like the old Roman). I had met Anthony a few months earlier at the PGA merchandise show, where he was scouting apparel for the Champions Tour's SAS Championship, for which he is a very dedicated volunteer. Ever since, we had kept in touch via texts and Facebook. The vibe was a little flirty, but he was coming to the Sybase as just a friend and die-hard golf fan. At least that was the idea. We spent a lot of time together during Anthony's three days at the tournament and I introduced him to a number of fellow players. As soon as we parted, my girlfriends would instantaneously BlackBerry messenger me something along the lines of "Who is that guy? You make such a cute couple!" I want to say that it was mostly because of the peer pressure that I started to develop feelings for Anthony. It seemed mutual, but shortly before his departure that Friday evening Anthony said something about his girlfriend back in North Carolina, a minor detail he had somehow neglected to mention up to that point. I was definitely surprised and a little let down.

The next morning my alarm went off at five A.M. for the second straight day and I couldn't shake a bummer mood. The weird good-bye with Anthony was probably a factor and the weather didn't help either: cold and wet and dreary. When I arrived at the course, my caddie Danny could tell I wasn't my usual cheerful self, but he's not the type to offer a rah-rah pep talk. My lack of spunk was definitely reflected in my play as I bogeyed four of the first eight holes en route to a miserable 75. There are so many highs and lows during a golf season, not all of them related to birdies and bogeys. The very best players can either block out the distractions or channel that energy into a

heightened focus: In 2004, while she was in the midst of expensive and unpleasant divorce proceedings, Annika Sorenstam
won eight tournaments and was Player of the Year. Even after all
these years I still sometimes struggle to find the right balance.
Emotion will always fuel my game, for better and for worse.

During the final round of the Sybase I was paired with Paige
MacKenzie, an ebullient, chatty young player. We spent the
whole round engrossed in conversation about boys and along
the way I shot a 71 that left me in thirty-seventh place. After the
final round Anthony sent me a text thanking me for all of the
hospitality. Whatever.

A primary topic of conversation at the player summit the week
before the Sybase was the tour's efforts to broaden our fan base,
and one of the tools the LPGA officials encouraged the players
to use was Twitter, the microblogging Web site that allows you
to post a running diary of your life, 140 characters at a time. A
handful of players were already habitual tweeters, including my
friend Morgan Pressel, always an early adopter of any new technology. Morgan had always beseeched me to use Twitter but I
resisted, because with my addictive personality I had a feeling it
would more or less take over my life. Following the summit I finally broke down and established my own feed and, as feared, it
didn't take me long to become obsessed. I started posting
dozens of daily tweets and corresponding with hundreds and
then thousands of followers. At the summit the LPGA officials
had talked about using Twitter to help us "build our brand."
There's no doubt that, as an institution, the LPGA needs to be
more creative in generating buzz because we don't get nearly

the same amount of coverage in print or on the airwaves as the PGA Tour. But for me Twitter was not clever viral marketing but rather a fun diversion and a dynamic way to interact with fans. From the Corning Classic, the tournament that immediately followed the Sybase, I did a giveaway for the lucky person who became my one thousandth follower, promising to send them a signed photo and a dozen golf balls. (I later repeated this for the two thousandth and three thousandth.) I also offered prizes to any follower who could correctly identify my favorite *South Park* episode of the season. Four people earned a box of balls for picking the very politically incorrect show "The Coon."

Being a touring pro can be an isolating life and Twitter is a way to feel connected to a larger community of like-minded people. I expressed my wonderment about modern technology in a tweet and was surprised and delighted when Davis Love III, the PGA Tour star, sent me a reply saying, "I remember back in the day before cell phones we had to wait outside the locker room for a pay phone to call home. Life is so grand now." Within a couple weeks of the summit so many LPGA players were tweeting that Bloomberg News did an item about the phenomenon. Noting that it was a great way to engage younger fans, LPGA commissioner Carolyn Bivens singled out the contributions of my busy fingers, saying, "If we're going to make golf chic, hip, happening, Christina Kim is exactly the kind of player to reach out and make golf a lot more relevant."

The drive from the Sybase Classic to the tiny town of Corning, in upstate New York, was pretty melancholy. After thirty-one years this was to be the final Corning Classic, ending one of the LPGA's most endearing and enduring events. The eponymous title sponsor, a maker of glass and ceramic products, had been hit hard by the economic downturn and gone through a series of layoffs. We all understood that underwriting a golf tournament didn't make sense in that context. The town of Corning has a population of only about eleven thousand, so there wasn't much in the way of other corporate support. The mom-and-pop scope that ultimately doomed the Corning Classic is the very thing that made it such a treasured experience for the players. For one week a year, the town and the tournament were basically the same thing. (On Main Street, a hand-operated leaderboard was always set up so folks could keep track of the scores while running errands.) We were embraced like part of an extended family, and all the players let down their guard and went out of their way to get to know the locals. It wasn't uncommon for a number of the very loyal volunteers to bring us homemade treats, and this year one older gent wrote a poem about me in microscopic print on a golf tee and offered it as a parting gift. Only in Corning. Through the years, we said that a lot.

After all the tributes and teary hugs throughout the early part of the week it was finally time to play some golf. The Corning Country Club is a classic, old-style course with twisty fairways and probably the smallest greens we play all year. During the first round I was swinging at it great, but I couldn't get any putts to fall. I hit so many lips I thought I was going to get herpes. Still, after birdying the par-5 twelfth hole I was three under par and cruising, feeling as though a strong finish would allow me to keep up with some very low scoring. (By the end of the day twenty-three players would post five under or better.) My round unraveled with one bad shot from the middle of the thirteenth fairway. I pushed a 9-iron well right of the green, leading to a bogey. All of a sudden I went from being comfortably under par to feeling anxious about needing to make more birdies. That just put more pressure on my putting, and I could feel the tension creeping into my stroke. I made nothing coming in, and a sloppy bogey on the eighteenth hole left me with a one-under 71, in a tie for seventy-second place. I stomped directly to the practice putting green for three hours of work, trying to improve the pace of my putts and just really needing to hear the sound of the ball going in the hole.

Hoping to change my luck, I put in play for the second round a new putter made by Kramski, a little outfit out of Germany that produces handmade beauties that are popular on the European Tour. This was my fourth putter of the year. At some point a more rational person might conclude the stroke was the problem, not the wand, but I wasn't ready to go there yet. I had long considered putting to be metaphysical, a kind of black art that defies any technical explanation. To me putting had nothing to do with mechanics but was all about the mystical, ephemeral "feel." Unfortunately, the putter swap didn't do me much good during the second round, which began on the tenth hole. Again I hit it nicely but couldn't convert enough opportunities. A tap-in birdie at number eighteen put me back to two under, which from studying the leaderboards I could tell would be the cut line. Since both par-5s on the front side are reachable for me, I just told myself to treat the final nine holes like a par-34, avoid any mistakes, and I would be fine. On the par-5 second hole I ripped my second shot, a 6-iron, to the center of the green . . . and then promptly three-putted for a disappointing par. I missed a fifteen-footer for birdie on number three and an eight-footer on number four. At the fifth hole a sweet 4-iron gave me another eagle opportunity, from thirty-five feet . . . and I three-putted again. I was so frustrated I wanted to kick a puppy, but somehow I kept producing quality shots. On the sixth hole I stuck my approach to five feet . . . and whiffed the putt. It's mentally exhausting when you're putting so poorly, and I made a couple of killer mistakes on the par-3 seventh hole. I chose the wrong club for my tee shot, leaving my ball on the front of the green, thirty-five feet from a hole cut on the top tier. It was a really tough putt and I didn't commit to rapping it firmly up the hill, leaving it six feet short. Of course I missed the ensuing par putt, taking a bogey that dropped me to one under. I knew I needed to play the final two holes under par to make the cut.

Standing over a twenty-five-foot birdie putt on the eighth hole, I had only one thought: Get it to the freaking hole and give yourself a chance. I left it four feet short. On number nine, a sharp dogleg right, I pushed my drive and was stymied by trees. I did well to slash a recovery shot to the edge of the green. I needed to chip in for a birdie and salvation. Naturally, I left the chip twelve feet short. Proving the golf gods have a sense of humor, I actually holed the twelve-footer for par, my sixty-ninth putt over two rounds. (Anything more than thirty putts in a round is pretty shabby.)

Normally when I miss the cut at a tournament I'm anxious to blow town as soon as possible, but this time I stuck around an extra day because Saturday night was to be Morgan Pressel's twenty-first birthday party. People have had the wrong idea about Morgan ever since the 2005 U.S. Women's Open, when she was a precocious seventeen-year-old amateur. You may recall that Morgan was tied for the lead standing in the seventy-second fairway when, up ahead, Birdie Kim thinned a shot out of the bunker, her ball clanging off the flagstick and into the hole for the unlikely birdie that ultimately won her the championship. Watching Kim's ball disappear, Morgan reacted as most teenagers would: She was totally miffed, kicking at the turf and not trying to hide her disappointment. But that bit of spontaneous emotion doesn't capture who she is. Morgan is an old soul, having lost her mom to breast cancer when she was fifteen. She's smart, witty, very down-to-earth, and also a huge sports fan who has single-handedly turned me into a hockey lover, and a lover of hockey players. Of course, being a blonde-haired, blue-eyed cutie-pie with a glam Polo wardrobe among her lucrative endorsement portfolio makes Morgan the object of a little jealousy. But to know her is to adore her, and ours is one of the friendships that has been strengthened in the wake of my breakup with Mark as I have tried so much harder to reconnect with the girls on tour.

A dozen players showed up for Morgan's birthday dinner. The only good thing about missing the cut was that I could party like a rock star while most of the other girls had to worry about getting up the next morning for the final round. (Morgan was on the leaderboard and thus nursed diet sodas throughout the evening.) At every gathering like this there has to be someone who makes an ass of herself, and I'm always happy to be that person. In fact, I'll get competitive about it. At this party

Yani Tseng was trying to steal my spotlight, going so far as to bust out a few handstands on the dance floor, so I had to work hard to make an even bigger ass of myself. One by one all the goody two-shoes begged off to get their precious sleep—to her credit, Yani got just enough rest to go out and win the next day—but I closed down the place along with Meaghan Francella, another player who was lucky to have missed the cut.

The next day I flew home to Orlando. There was no tournament the week after Corning, so I had time to tune up my game. Little did I know it would turn into a major overhaul.

To this point in the season I had spent a lot of energy trying to find myself as a person. Now I needed to focus on relocating my golf game. Since I was struggling with my putting, I decided the logical thing to do was change my clubs, my ball, and my swing. Actually, I had been contemplating all of these moves for a while, and my lackluster play since the Dinah Shore convinced me the time had arrived. Swapping balls wasn't too big a deal; I went from the Titleist Pro-V1x to a Bridgestone Tour B330-S. On the launch monitor the numbers were virtually identical, but I liked the Bridgestone's seamless cover technology. The Pro-V1x's cover is two separate half spheres that are joined during the manufacturing process, creating an invisible seam down the middle. It's a great ball, but every once in a great while I'd get one that seemed a little lopsided.

Changing irons was much more traumatic. I've always experimented with the latest drivers, putters, and wedges, but for my entire pro career—and, in fact, this entire millennium—I've used the same model of Henry-Griffitts blades. It's not a really well-known brand, but the HGs are handmade custom clubs popular among elite players. It was such a big deal when I got my first set at age fourteen, and I'd always been extremely reluctant to stray even as more forgiving, technologically advanced clubs became common on tour. But I began tinkering with a set of TaylorMade Tour Preferreds and found that my good shots were about the same—but on mis-hits the TaylorMades performed much, much better. Feeling like I needed all the help I could get, I retired my Henry-Griffitts with a very heavy heart. Completing the equipment overhaul, I went with steel shafts (ninety-five-gram KDS, stiff), whereas I'd always had graphite in my irons.

My big swing change was to keep my left arm straighter on the backswing. I was letting it collapse going back, which left the clubface open at the top and forced me to do a little Sergio loop on the way down to square the face. I've toyed with a straighter left arm for years, but this time I was committed to sticking with the change. Just a little tweak of one arm doesn't sound like a lot, but any time you mess with your mechanics it feels awkward and unnatural, like trying to write with the wrong hand. I struggled for days to groove my new action. Still, I was encouraged with the progress, as was my dad, who stood vigil by my side throughout the week. He's the only teacher I've ever trusted, going back to a scarring experience when I was sixteen. In search of an experienced instructor, I went to the Butch Harmon School of Golf for a long weekend, and one of Butch's lieutenants messed me up so terribly it took months before I could hit the ball solidly again. After that Dad and I have never trusted anyone else with my swing.

Finally it was time to test out the new me in competition, at the LPGA State Farm Classic in Springfield, Illinois. The State Farm's host venue, Panther Creek Country Club, has always been a good golf course for me because it has pretty wide fairways and, at 6,746 yards, it's one of the two or three longest tracks we play all year. Arriving on the first tee for my first round I had some serious butterflies because of all the uncertainty with my sticks and my swing. Back-to-back birdies on six and seven settled me down a bit, but I made a costly mistake on the ninth hole. With my "old" swing, my miss was a snipe low and left. With my new action, I was still figuring out what kind of bad shot I needed to guard against. The ninth is a cape hole with a drive over water; the farther right you aim, the longer the carry. I took an aggressive line but then uncorked a weak fade. It was the wrong swing on the wrong hole, and my drive splashed into the lake. Double bogey.

The next hole was key. I regrouped on the tee and smashed a drive down the middle, then followed with a lovely knockdown 8-iron to three feet for a much-needed birdie. Having such perfect distance control gave me a shot of confidence and I made two more birds coming for a hard-fought 72, even par but hardly routine.

Friday was my cleanest round in a good long while, a 68 built on five birdies and a lone bogey. I was loving my new irons and feeling good about my swing. The positive vibes carried over to the third round, at least for a while. I played the first ten holes in −3 and was just cruising along until I nuked a gap wedge over the twelfth green, leading to a bogey. It's amazing how quickly confidence can evaporate, and that one bad shot spooked me to the core. Suddenly I didn't trust my swing, or my ability to hit the ball the correct distance. Instead of attacking the remaining holes I began playing defensively, trying to steer my ball away from the bunkers and other hazards. This kind of meek golf always leads to trouble. I made some shaky pars and a messy bogey on the easy par-5 sixteenth hole (which I would birdie every other round) for a very disappointing 71. I had a weird feeling of being all alone out there, as my caddie Danny couldn't quite find the words to help me out of my back-nine funk. I'd had this feeling a few other times during the season, and as far back as the Phoenix LPGA International, in March, I had considered making a caddie change. It hadn't happened yet because I was afraid of the upheaval, but that night, analyzing my awful back nine, I again began to think it might be time to have a different personality carrying my bag.

Remember how at the Sybase Classic, two weeks earlier, I struggled emotionally during that flat 75? Sunday at the State Farm was the flipside. I wasn't hitting it that great but my playing partners got me so fired up I produced some of my most inspired golf of the season to date. Yani Tseng birdied six of the first twelve holes and Eunjung Yi birdied seven of the first sixteen, and I sure as hell wasn't going to let them show me up so I made six birdies of my own. After a good drive on the eighteenth hole I was thinking of trying to snag one more but I hit another weak fade, and this one also drowned in a greenside hazard. Bummer thoughts flooded my brain. The first was, there go some precious Solheim points. These accrue over the course of the year, awarded for each top-twenty finish. Before making double bogey, I was in good position to score a fistful of points. This would've solidified my number-six spot on the U.S. rankings with another month and a half left to go in the qualifying period; with the missed opportunity, I was suddenly aware of the precariousness of my position. The next thought was, there goes a bunch of money. Over the course of seventy-two holes, every stroke is equally important, but when you screw up the eighteenth hole on Sunday you're more aware of the financial implications. A birdie at eighteen would have lifted me to fifteenth place, good for about $24,000. Instead, that double bogey dropped me to twenty-seventh, worth $14,097. That's an expensive mistake.

Once I cooled off from my final-hole blunder I was pretty pleased with how the week went, given all the change I was dealing with. As usual with me, there was a little intrigue off the course, too. From the State Farm I traveled to Havre de Grace, Maryland, for the LPGA Championship, the second major championship of the year. My first night there, on Monday, I met up with a guy named Jeff with whom I had been exchanging tweets for the previous couple of weeks, including some feverish correspondence in the preceding few days. He seemed really smart and funny and, since he lived in nearby Baltimore, it was like, why not? The rendezvous spot was a well-lit public place, in this case a suburban mall. I could have made history as the first LPGA player to enjoy a hookup through Twitter, but instead we just strolled around the mall chatting. The vibe was friendly and cordial, but that's as far as it went, as the evening ended with nothing more than a courtesy hug.

My big mouth has gotten me in trouble plenty of times, but for the LPGA Championship it brought me a lot of extra attention, most of it positive. The Golf Channel asked me to wear a microphone for the first round, and I was thrilled and flattered.

Everyone else was greatly amused, especially at the prospect of four-letter words being spewed live on the airwaves. I had to explain to various friends and colleagues that this season I was already making a concerted effort to watch my language and that there would be no R-rated slipups. I was actually a little insulted—did people really think I used to be so vulgar?

Tee times for the first two rounds of every tournament are supposedly created by an unfeeling computer, but sometimes you have to wonder. For Thursday and Friday I was paired with Michelle Wie. Her rookie year was off to a fast start—three top tens to that point in the season—and she had quickly reestablished herself as the LPGA's biggest draw. So the cameras following me would also get to record her every twitch, too. A mean-spirited item in *GolfWeek* later suggested that by wearing the microphone I wasn't taking a major championship seriously enough. Lame! If anything, the extra attention only made me more determined to play my best. I also had history on my side, having worn a microphone once before, at the 2005 Tournament of Champions, a tournament I won. Before the first round, a Golf Channel technician attached the battery pack to the waistband of my skirt and helped me snake the cords under my shirt. (That was the most action I'd had in a while!) Wearing the gear felt comfortable and familiar; for years I had carried a yardage guide in my back pocket, and it weighed about the same as the battery.

At major championships I've always had a tendency to try too hard, so I spent the practice rounds just trying to be mellow and treat it like any other week. I felt surprisingly relaxed stepping to the first tee for the first round and I played a pretty solid front nine, turning in one over. On eleven I rolled in a twenty-footer for birdie, punctuated by a whoop that probably startled a few viewers at home. I birdied thirteen after a killer 4-iron to eight feet. A bogey out of the rough on sixteen was offset by another bird at seventeen, leaving me with a 71. I was quite pleased—anything under par at a major championship is always a good start.

Michelle also played well, firing a 70, and we enjoyed our usual good chemistry, chitchatting about a variety of things including the general hotness of hockey players. I tend to haze Michelle like a kid sister, and this day was no exception. She's so tall with such a hard body, I began referring to her as a "gangly giraffe," which seemed to amuse the Golf Channel commentators, Dottie Pepper and Brian Hammons. I always find Michelle to be witty and fun, but most people only get to see her grim game face, so the first-round coverage was good for both of us: Many people tweeted that they had no idea how cool she is. In fact, by the time I checked that evening, I had over four hundred comments through Twitter. Buoyed by all the love, I wrote back to every single person that night. The positive feedback the Golf Channel execs received was enough for them to ask me to wear the mike again for the second round, and I happily agreed. Unfortunately, I didn't play nearly as well.

Starting on the back nine, I bogeyed the twelfth hole, but it wasn't a bad bogey, considering I got up and down after dumping my approach into a hazard. I followed with another bogey at thirteen after pushing a 4-iron into a greenside bunker. On the sixteenth hole I hit a perfect 3-wood off the tee but my drive settled into a nasty divot. I was beginning to feel as though it wasn't going to be my day, but I was determined to keep grinding. After duffing my approach short of the green, I played a perfect bump and run that tumbled into the hole for a birdie. I thoroughly enjoyed the round of high fives from my playing partners, but the momentum quickly evaporated when I bogeyed the seventeenth hole from a greenside bunker. So I was two over par on my round making the turn. I studied the leaderboard and couldn't believe the low scores—were these girls playing the same golf course? I was still in good position to make the cut, but if I wanted to contend on the weekend I would have to get going.

A sweet birdie on number two was neutralized by a three-putt bogey on four. The par-4 sixth hole was a killer. I pushed my drive into the rough and the lie was so thick all I could do was hack the ball out in the general direction of the green. Unluckily, it scooted into a gaping greenside bunker. I felt so lost as I was walking down the fairway, like, What is wrong with me? I was trying so hard but I couldn't get anything going. Now I faced a brutal sand shot, a forty-yard carry to a back pin. I thought I hit it pretty well, but my ball carried only thirty-nine yards, catching the lip of the bunker and falling back in. I splashed out and then missed a twelve-foot putt. The ghastly double bogey pushed me to three over for the tournament, which I was pretty sure would be the cut line. Pars on seven and eight set up a do-or-die thirty-sixth hole. I hit a good drive into the wind but still had 176 yards in. Trying to smash a 5-iron, I pulled it a bit into a gnarly patch of rough, leaving me a downhill, sidehill shot to a tucked pin. I grinded so hard over the ensuing flop shot and hit a beauty to four feet. So two long days of golf came down to one putt. Make it or go home. I didn't make it.

After all the pomp with the Golf Channel, the ending was pretty unceremonious. A staffer met me behind the green to reclaim the mike. He thanked me for being a good sport, and that was that.

Suicidal is too strong a word—barely—but I was pretty distraught after the round. Shooting 77 to miss the cut in a big tournament is a bummer under any circumstance. To do it with the whole world watching—at least that's how it felt—was a huge blow to my pride. I returned to my hotel room and curled into the fetal position on the bed, feeling awful about myself. Then I got a much-needed phone call from Meg Mallon, the beloved veteran who has always been such a generous mentor to me. That night happened to be game seven of the Stanley Cup finals, and a handful of girls were gathering to watch it at a sports bar. Surmising my mental state, Meg insisted I join them. I almost walked out the door caked in sweat and still in my grubby golf togs, but I decided that to change my mood I needed to change my appearance. So I dolled myself up with plenty of makeup, a little black dress, and a pair of very sexy Manolo Blahnik heels. As soon as I walked in the door and spied my table of friends, my first thought was, Boy, am I glad I showered! Meg had brought along her nephew Dan, with whom I'd had a little flirtation four years earlier.

It happened at the 2005 Solheim Cup, at which Meg and I were teammates. Not long after making the Cup-clinching putt, Meg grew faint and felt as if her heart was beating irregularly, so she was taken to the hospital as a precaution. (Imagine how she would have felt if she had missed the putt!) I went to visit, and at the sight of her in bed with tubes in her arms I completely lost it. I had never met Dan before, but he was so comforting and sweet, getting me to laugh through my tears. (It didn't hurt that he was cute, too.) We talked on the phone after that, but once things got serious with my boyfriend Mark I fell out of touch with Dan, though I must admit I thought about him every now and then. Even though my beloved Red Wings lost a classic game seven—actually, they're Morgan Pressel's team and I had merely jumped on the bandwagon—I had a great time talking and flirting with Dan. We resolved to keep in better touch this time around.

The next day I nursed a mild hangover and spent a lot of time reflecting on what had been ailing my golf game. The bad play was entirely my responsibility, but I also came to the conclusion that I didn't have the right wingman out there as my caddie. I continued stewing on this during a dinner with an old friend named Alexandra. As I was sitting at the restaurant I made up my mind to pull the trigger on firing my caddie Danny Wilson, a move I had been considering for a while. Danny is an excellent bagman, very astute with the club selection and strategy and all of the little nuances that are so important to his job. But he's a very laid-back, soft-spoken guy, and I was realizing I needed a more energetic, enthusiastic voice to help keep me focused and fire me up when things aren't going my way.

A caddie is one of the most important people in the life of any professional golfer. They're equal parts psychologist, swing coach, strategist, and wet nurse. During a tournament week, most players spend more waking hours with their caddie than with any other person, including their significant other. A player's needs are very idiosyncratic; some girls have their caddie read every putt and check their alignment before every swing. I'm pretty independent, preferring to crunch my own yardage numbers and eye my own putts. I rely on my caddie more for company than anything else. Danny is a really nice guy, but he's twice my age, and ultimately we stopped clicking.

Hiring and firing caddies is one of the hardest parts of tour life, especially for a young player. Suddenly you're a businesswoman responsible for the livelihood of another person, and there's no training for this delicate role. Because my dad caddied for me over the first four years of my career I had canned only one non–family member, Donna Southam, the caddie who preceded Danny. Donna and I worked together for most of 2007 and had some nice success, but we never won a tournament. It's hard to describe why, but I just felt as though I would have trouble winning with her on the bag. Walking up to Donna to tell her it was over, I was shaking with nerves. Hearing me stutter and stammer, she finally said, "It's okay, honey, just say it." I'll always be grateful to her for being so classy.

For the sake of both of our careers, I had to break the bad news to Danny as soon as possible so he could start looking for a new bag and I could try to find his replacement. Unfortunately, my dinner with Alexandra had dragged on well past nine o'clock and the restaurant was an hour away from where Danny was staying. I was too worn-out to drive to his hotel and back, so I decided to do the deed over the phone. I felt horrible about it; telling someone they're losing their job is the kind of thing that should be done face-to-face. Danny is a good person and he definitely deserved better. My fingers were shaking as I dialed his number, and as soon as I heard his voice my heart was in my throat. But Danny's a pro and he knows this is part of life on tour. He was incredibly gracious and kind, and the conversation went about as well as possible. As tacky as it was to fire Danny by phone, I guess there's a silver lining: At least I didn't do it via Twitter.

New swing, new equipment, new boys, no caddie, same old results—did this constitute progress? I wasn't so sure. But I was determined to figure out my life on and off the course. That means not being afraid of change, however scary it may be.

CHAPTER 7

Dollars and Sense

O n June 20, six days after the conclusion of the LPGA Championship, I journeyed to Providence to play in the pro-am of the CVS Charity Classic, the tournament run by Brad Faxon and Billy Andrade, native sons of Rhode Island who have enjoyed long careers on the PGA Tour. It's a really fun little event that supports a number of local charities, and I was honored to be asked to participate. I have to admit I was also lured by the $7,500 appearance fee. I used to play a dozen or so outings a year like this to earn some extra folding money. The minimum I'd take was $5K, while the most I ever got was $12,500—not Paula Creamer money (America's sweetheart earned a reported $1 million to play in a Japanese LPGA event earlier in the year) but still a pretty great wage for one round of golf. With domestic corporate dollars drying up due to the de-pressed economy, the CVS was the first appearance fee I had cashed all year.

From Providence I made the lovely six-hour drive across

Massachusetts and much of New York State to the city of Rochester for the Wegmans LPGA. It's one of the best tournaments of the year, boasting a phenomenal golf course and huge community support. The first order of business was to get my caddie situation in order. When firing your looper it's advisable to have a replacement already lined up, but parting ways with Danny had been pretty spontaneous so I was still scrambling. Word of a caddie firing travels at the speed of light—or, at the very least, the speed of text messaging—and during the off week prior to the Wegmans I had expected to be wooed by any number of enterprising caddies. But all I got were a couple of lousy texts. Obviously it hadn't been a great year for me so far, but July is the heart of the schedule with three big-money events: the U.S. Women's Open, the Evian Masters, and the Women's British Open. I was also still in prime position to make the Solheim Cup team, at seventh in the points race. So I was a little miffed that hardly any caddies inquired about the job, and I definitely started doubting myself: *Do people think I'm a sucky golfer? Do I have B.O.?*

Things started to percolate once I got settled in at Locust Hill Country Club, site of the Wegmans. (And not just for me—I was cheered to hear that Danny had no trouble finding a new bag.) On that Tuesday, Dave Brooker committed to caddie for me at the U.S. Women's Open, to be played two weeks after the Wegmans. He couldn't do it sooner because he was nursing a foot injury sustained in a pickup soccer game. Brooker was limping proof of how fickle the caddie game can be: He had been let go a few weeks earlier by Lorena Ochoa even though they had won a couple dozen tournaments together in the preceding four years. Lorena was still number one in the world ranking, but she was mired in one of the longest funks of her career and wanted to make a change for the sake of change, so good-bye Dave. He has a wife and three daughters to support, so I told him that if a great long-term option became available I would understand if he had to bail on me. Sure enough, the very next morning he called to say he had just been offered Suzann Pettersen's bag and she wanted him to start at the Open. I couldn't blame Dave for kicking me to the curb, considering Suzann is one of the two or three best players in the game. He suggested I contact a caddie named Jason Hamilton, who is known far and wide as Donny because he bears a striking resemblance to the old Australian pop singer Donny Hamilton.

I was friendly with Donny from years earlier, when he had worked for Suzann Pettersen, Helen Alfredsson, and Mi Hyun Kim. In recent seasons he had been concentrating on the men's tour, including stints with big-time players like Y. E. Yang, Paul Casey, and Anthony Kim. Donny was looking for work because his most recent bag, Tim Wilkinson, was suddenly out with an injury. After a flurry of texts, Donny agreed to work for me. I was over the moon because he's a young, ambitious, hungry, confident guy, and he said he was eager to help me with my game and get me to reach my full potential. The only minor sticking point was his pay. I offered him one thousand dollars a tournament and the standard 5-7-10 split, which meant he would take 5 percent of my winnings, with that number bumped to 7 percent for a top-ten finish and 10 percent of a victory check. Donny wanted eleven hundred a week. I was willing to do that, but made a counteroffer: If he were to settle for the one thousand, we could do a 6-8-11 split. This was Donny's first test—of both his ability to crunch numbers and his confidence in me. Considering that a first-place check can be worth upward of two hundred thousand dollars, that extra 1 percent could be worth two grand or more. Was he really willing to give up that potential payday in exchange for an extra hundred bucks? I was relieved when Donny went for the thousand dollars and the 6-8-11 percentages. One thing I didn't count on was his power of persuasion, or my eagerness to please; by the end of our negotiations, I had agreed to give him the 6-8-11 plus eleven hundred a tournament. So much for my hardball negotiating skills.

By the time all of this got sorted out Donny was already committed to caddying for another player at the Wegmans, so I needed an emergency looper to get me through the week. When I summoned my dad he tried to play it cool but I could tell how excited he was. I know in his mind we were going to win the tournament, I would insist he be my full-time caddie until the end of time, and things would go back to how they used to be. It took all of three holes of the first round for both of us to realize that the good old days were long gone. It was a very hot day, and strolling down the third fairway I looked back and was startled to see the old man lagging eighty yards behind. When he finally huffed up to the green he was drenched in sweat, and I spent the rest of the round fretting that he was going to keel over.

Part of Dad's problem was that he had gained a few extra pounds; my struggles at the Wegmans were a by-product of all the weight I had lost. In the two months since my sojourn to Korea, the pounds had continued to melt away and I was almost down to a size 7. I was jogging five miles at least five days a week, propelled by an iPod playlist entitled "Run, Bitch, Run."

The only downside to all those disappearing pounds is that suddenly I was driving it like a twelve-year-old girl. My long balls off the tee always owed more to my sheer mass than to flawless technique. But now I had lost twenty-five pounds and it seemed like just as many yards. So for the first round of the Wegmans I decided to ditch my TaylorMade driver and go with a new Callaway. The experiment was a disaster. Locust Hill is a tight, tree-lined course, and I spent the entire round in the woods. Crafty scrambling on the front nine allowed me to salvage a one-over 37, but on the tenth hole I blew my drive into the trees on the right and made bogey. On the par-5 eleventh I drove it way left into a forest and then misplayed a punch-out with my 4-iron, forcing me to chip another shot out into the fairway. I knocked my fourth onto the green, leaving twelve feet to save par. Instead I gunned the putt way by the hole and then missed the comebacker, leading to a horrific double bogey. Poor Dad. He was so bewildered, muttering over and over, "What are you doing?" On the thirteenth tee he offered a little advice: "Try hitting straight." Like I hadn't thought of that already! A chip-in for birdie on the eighteenth hole left me with a 75 and a woebegone 107th place.

For the second round I went back to my old r9 and drove it much better, setting up birdies on three of the first eight holes. (I began my round on the tenth tee.) Dad couldn't contain his excitement, at one point saying, "There you go, so much better! I knew could do it!"

After a long rain delay, we ran out of daylight with five holes left to complete the round. That night I went to dinner with some other players and shared a few funny stories about my dad's return to caddying. Having him on the bag definitely brought back some great memories. After a couple of shots, he had bellowed his heavily accented version of *perfect*: "PUH-fec!" That always brought a smile to my face, just as it had all those years ago. I was feeling so warm and fuzzy toward my dad until I returned to the Residence Inn, where we were sharing a two-bedroom suite. When Dad is on the road with me I try to find a place to stay with a kitchen because we enjoy cooking for each other and it bothers him to pay restaurant prices. On this night he had found some kind of frozen-fish thingy at a Korean grocer. He put it straight in the oven, and I think the excessive steam set off the hotel's fire alarm. I was sitting on my bed when this happened, and, stealing a peek out the window, I could see dozens of grumpy players gathered outside in various states of undress, trying to identify the culprit. There was no way I was going to leave the room, as I was more likely to die of embarrassment than smoke inhalation. Eventually the firemen arrived and allowed everyone back in around ten thirty P.M. The hotel manager called the room to express his dismay, but he failed to realize that Koreans love a good argument and Dad quickly turned it around, saying, "Something is wrong with you stupid oven and you stupid fire alarm. My food not even fully cooked—how can I start a fire? I stand here and wait for someone to come and look at my food!" It was classic.

The next morning the second round was restarted at seven A.M. I arrived at the course by five forty-five but still felt like I didn't get to warm up properly. My first hole was the par-3 fifth, and, even though it was a solid strike, my tee shot came up thirty-five feet short, which after the fact I realized was a result of the heavy early-morning air. Then I failed to take into account how the dew would slow the greens, so my putt expired eight feet short of the hole. I missed the ensuing par putt, pushing me to the precipice of another missed cut. I needed to play the final four holes in no worse than even par.

On the sixth hole, my 4-iron approach drifted left of the green and I couldn't get up and down, leading to another bogey. With my dad on the bag there was no way I was going to stop fighting, so after a great par save on number seven I hit a series of perfect shots on the final two holes. But both birdie tries, from around fifteen feet, lipped out. My 72 was two strokes too many, and for the first time since 2004 I had missed two consecutive cuts. Having those birdie putts lip out was such a heartbreaker that by the time the scorecards were signed I was sobbing and there was nothing my caddie could do to comfort me.

Missing cuts is a blow to your pride and also your wallet. There are no guaranteed contracts for pro golfers. We have to kill what we eat. Missing the cut means you don't earn a cent for that week even as you have to shell out for airfare, hotel, rental car, gas, meals, caddie fees, iTunes downloads, and innumerable other little expenses. The Wegmans had a two-million-dollar purse, a number exceeded by only three nonmajors. Inbee Park went 75-81 on the weekend to finish DFL—dead fucking last— but she still earned $3,833, more than enough to at least cover costs in an inexpensive city like Rochester. (Jiyai Shin, the bubbly young superstar from Korea, banked three hundred thousand dollars for her victory.)

It was during the week of the Wegmans that I booked my upcoming European trip for the Evian Masters, in the French

Alps, and the Women's British, at Royal Lytham & St. Annes Golf Club in Lancashire, England. For limited-field events like Thailand and Singapore at the start of the year, the tournament picks up airfare, but Evian and the British are full field, so I spent twenty-five hundred dollars on the ticket plus forty thousand frequent-flier miles to upgrade to business class. Going overseas I always fly business because the comfier seats, better food, and general pampering help me feel more refreshed when I arrive and have to go to work. Usually I can buy a coach ticket and upgrade with miles. Still, I've kicked down as much as fifty-five hundred dollars on airfare in the past. My attitude is, you gotta spend it to make it. I paid another eight hundred for Donny's ticket to the Evian. Most players in, say, the top thirty of the money list spring for their caddie's airfare. It's all negotiable, and even though to this point in the season I was languishing outside the top fifty, I was confident that Donny would help my game. To induce him to stick around, I offered to cover his airfare for the rest of the season.

In the U.S. my unofficial maximum for a hotel room is two hundred dollars a night. I'm very loyal to the Marriott chain so there's usually pretty good options, and in more expensive cities the LPGA will sometimes negotiate a group rate. Overseas hotels can be a lot pricier. Évian-les-Bains is a beautiful resort area, and all the hotel rooms were a painful $350 and up. For my week in England, my agent found a little inn that was surprisingly affordable, about two hundred dollars a night, including an artery-clogging English breakfast.

All in, I spend eighty to ninety thousand dollars a year on expenses, plus at least another sixty thousand on my caddie. When my dad was on my bag full-time he was one of the best-paid loopers on tour, with a salary of more than a hundred thousand dollars a year. I like my dad and all, but his bloated paycheck was really done to save me a bundle on taxes. My family's attitude toward money has always been what's mine is yours, so whatever I paid my dad just went back into one big pot for all of us to share. My mom remains on the payroll to act as my treasurer, handling all the bills and managing our accounts and helping to prepare the endless tax returns. (Like all touring pros, I have to file in every state in which I collect a check, which is as big a pain in the ass as it sounds like.)

Even though prize winnings are subject to the maddening vagaries of the game, my earnings have been remarkably consistent—from 2004 to 2008, I made between $620,000 and $680,000 every year except '06, when I slumped a bit and wound up cashing $355K. (In those years my ranking on the money list was, in order, fifteenth, nineteenth, thirty-fifth, twenty-third, and twenty-seventh.) The only significant endorsement money I've ever made came in '07 and '08, when the cell phone company V-Tech paid me $150,000 each year to wear their logo and make a few promotional appearances. There are plenty of players supporting big entourages made up of some combination of swing coach, short-game guru, personal trainer, sports psychologist, nutritionist, publicist, personal assistant, and assorted other hangers-on. I like to keep it in the family and limit my overhead. In 2008 I worked with Dr. Joseph Parent, the author of *Zen Golf.* He was very helpful in sharpening my mental approach, but after six months I felt like there was nothing left for me to learn so we parted ways. I don't need to spend five hundred dollars an hour to have someone hold my hand for the rest of my career.

Away from golf, my biggest monthly expense is my mortgage. In late 2004 my parents and I finally moved out of our apartment in San Jose after I bought a 3,500-square-foot, six-bedroom house for us to share in Orlando's Dr. Phillips neighborhood, at a price of six hundred thousand dollars. The real estate agent took us to see a bunch of houses and I liked them all, so I told my parents to pick. At twenty years old, what does anyone know about real estate? Anyway, I wanted Mom and Dad to be happy. They sacrificed so much for me growing up, so I'm thrilled to be able to take care of them now that they have both retired. I guess there's a little pressure to be the family's breadwinner, but I try not to think about it. Play good golf and everything will take care of itself.

My only other really big purchases have been automobiles. In 2005 I bought an Escalade and flossed it out with chrome rims and an eardrum-bursting sound system. I wanted to be a baller, but now I consider that oversized SUV to be an ostentatious gas hog and rarely drive it, preferring to bop around in my 2002 Civic hybrid. For Christmas 2008 I surprised my parents with a Mercedes-Benz E550. It was a bit extravagant, but I was so happy to do it for them.

When it comes to spending money, my only real vice has been shoes. I have at least seventy pairs, including a dozen Manolo Blahniks, ten Jimmy Choos, five Dolce & Gabbanas, twenty Stuart Weitzmans, and $3,500 Giuseppe Zanotti cowboy boots from the cowgirl phase I went through in 2006 and don't really care to discuss. On the LPGA Tour there is a cult of handbags, but my collection is not too outrageous: only about fifteen, and only one really crazy purchase, a Jimmy Choo python bag that set me back about $4,500.

Traditionally I have celebrated every top-ten tournament finish with a little splurging, but this year I've stopped treating Saks Fifth Avenue like it's Costco. Part of that was my slow start to the year—through the Wegmans I had earned $117,113—but it was also a nod to the overall financial climate on tour. With our schedule contracting due to corporate belt-tightening, all of us were feeling a little uncertain about the future, and I had noticed a lot less conspicuous consumption among the girls. (Some players had become so cost conscious, they were sharing hotel rooms and rental cars.) Casual fans seem to think that playing professional golf is easy money, but that's just the PGA Tour, the land of the haves and have-mores, where struggling means having to settle for a Porsche instead of a Ferrari. In 2009 Kevin Streelman finished ninety-first on the PGA Tour money list, earning $1,007,444. Jennifer Rosales was ninety-first on the LPGA money list, making $92,832. Factor in expenses and you can literally go broke playing the LPGA Tour unless you're in the top fifty or so of the money list.

I've saved enough through the years to allow me to weather the occasional minislump, but the back-to-back missed cuts definitely hurt. I've always played my best golf—and made most of my money—in the second half of the year, so that gave me a little peace of mind. The week after the Wegmans brought the Jamie Farr Owens Corning Classic in Toledo, Ohio, the exact midpoint of the schedule: the fourteenth tournament of the year, out of twenty-seven. It was time to start paying the bills.

*　　*　　*　　*

The Jamie Farr is a nice little event with a strong emphasis on aiding local charities. The eponymous host always makes an appearance, although sadly he's never turned out in drag like his most famous character, Corporal Klinger from *M*A*S*H**. On Monday of that week I finally hooked up with my new caddie, Donny, for a pro-am. Before the round I was on the practice putting green and the first thing he said to me was, "Are you trying to stand that way?"

I didn't realize I looked like a contortionist taking the putter back, with my hips and shoulders way too open and far too much weight on my left side. Even for touring pros, bad posture and misalignment can incrementally creep into our game. I guess it took a fresh set of eyes to see my problems. Donny has been on the men's tour, he's been around great players, he sees things a certain way, and he's not afraid to speak his mind. I have total confidence in him, so I followed his orders as he coached me how to improve my posture and square my stance. Suddenly I started pouring in putts. Not only was the ball going in, but it was rolling beautifully end over end, hugging the ground. Honestly, this was the first time in my career that putting practice was enjoyable. All I could say to Donny was, Where have you been all my life?

Donny continued to help me with my game during the practice rounds. As the week wore on, I started to feel pressure to play well for him. I knew his heart was on the PGA Tour, but I felt as though some good results with me might convince him to stick around. My hopes of making a good impression were dashed a bit when I saw the pairings for the first two rounds. For the first time since my rookie year, I had been consigned to the so-called B Group. The A Group is made up

of sixty players, with a pecking order based on tournament winners from the previous two seasons, the top forty on the career
money list, and the current season's money list. Basically, these
are the most accomplished players in the field, and the B Group
is everybody else. The groups get reshuffled twice during the
season to take into account movement on the money list. Because of my mediocre play so far in 2009, I had been demoted.
There are competitive disadvantages to being B-listed, as you
get stuck with tee times that are earlier in the morning and
later in the afternoon. That means waking up in the dark one
day and playing late in the afternoon on another, when it's often windier and the greens are crustier and more beat-up from
spiked shoes and ball marks. There's also the psychological aspect. My ego was in so much pain when I discovered I had slid
to the B group, and it was pretty humbling to have to explain it
to Donny.

My first-round tee time for the Farr was eight twenty A.M., so
I set my iPhone alarm to five A.M. with my traditional wakeup
song, Jet's "Cold Hard Bitch." In all of my years of tournament
golf I'd never had a problem with my alarm. Until this day.
When I opened my eyes it was exactly six fifty-eight A.M. I was so
shocked I could barely breathe. Even though I was in full freak-
out mode, I still had to take a shower—otherwise I would have
felt weird and gross for the rest of the day. I got put together in
record time and made the twenty-minute drive to the course in
exactly thirteen minutes, my heart racing along with the engine
of my rental car. It was seven thirty-five when I screeched into
the player parking lot. Donny greeted me, and he was so sooth-
ing and mellow it helped me slow down and get focused. I still
went through my OCD preround practice routine of hitting

every club, though I only had enough time to hit a ball or two with each.

I started my round on the tenth tee and played so-so over the first eight holes, with seven pars and a bogey. On the par-5 eighteenth I laid up to within fifty-seven yards of the flag. It was an awkward yardage, so Donny kept telling me to visualize the shot before I hit it. That really helped me zero in on what I wanted to do. I put a beautiful strike on the ball and it landed right where I was aiming, took a couple of hops, and then disappeared into the cup for a stunning eagle. Donny and I shared a big hug and I was so fired up I immediately birdied the next hole, too. It was a pretty auspicious beginning to our partnership. There were no more pyrotechnics coming in, so my opening 70 left me in sixty-sixth place, not too bad considering the crazy start to the day.

When I arrived at the course for my Friday-afternoon tee time, everyone was buzzing about what had transpired the night before. A dozen top players—including, according to *GolfWeek*, Lorena Ochoa, Paula Creamer, Natalie Gulbis, Cristie Kerr, Juli Inkster, Suzann Pettersen, and Morgan Pressel—had gathered for an impromptu dinner at which they all vented their various grievances about LPGA commissioner Carolyn Bivens. Before the meal was over, a letter had been drafted to the LPGA's board of directors basically demanding a change in leadership. This insurrection had been brewing for a while, but what finally spurred the players to action was the announcement the day before that the Kapalua LPGA Classic, scheduled for October, was being canceled due to the lack of corporate sponsorship. That was the latest setback in what had been a string of bad financial news for the tour. The Jamie Farr was the third tournament in a row that did not yet have a sponsor in place for 2010, following the McDonald's LPGA Championship and the Wegmans LPGA, and that trifecta came just a few weeks after the Corning Classic went kaput.

LPGA players are not naïve. We were all very aware that the recession was forcing corporations to cut back their spending and that women's golf, as a niche sport, was vulnerable. That was made abundantly clear when five tournaments vanished from the 2009 schedule before the season even began. Throughout the year there had been numerous news stories detailing the shaky state of the tour, and many of these reports, whether fair or not, pointed the finger at Bivens for chasing away cost-conscious corporations with her hardball negotiating. The players' collective frustration finally boiled over in Toledo, putting her future in doubt.

Bivens had been named commissioner in 2005, plucked from a media-services company. She did not have a strong golf background and that was probably a good thing, because she did not reflexively accept the LPGA's traditional place on the margins of the golf world. Bivens sized up the tour's assets—young, telegenic, personable American talent; a deep pool of international stars; voracious foreign markets—and she embarked on an ambitious agenda. Her stated goals were to improve our television presence, increase purses, expand the schedule into key foreign markets, and upgrade the players' retirement benefits.

I supported all of these initiatives—pretty much every player did, and Bivens had some important victories. She successfully pushed sponsors to commit more money for purses and shoulder more of the tournament-operating costs. The LPGA expanded its tournament schedule in Asia and Mexico. While PGA Tour commissioner Tim Finchem dragged his feet, Bivens instituted the first performance-enhancing-drug testing policy in professional golf. Her biggest coup was forging a ten-year deal with the Golf Channel to become the LPGA's exclusive domestic cable broadcaster, beginning in 2010. A lot of our television coverage had been on ESPN2, where the LPGA wasn't a priority for the network and we got small broadcast windows and D-list announcers. The Golf Channel will provide more and better coverage and endless promotion. Importantly, the Golf Channel will also be compelled to broadcast more foreign events, as in 2009 five international tournaments received zero airtime in the U.S., including a thrilling Ochoa-Pettersen duel that went down to the last hole in Morelia, Mexico. The Golf Channel deal was announced at the 2009 season opener, at which Bivens also trumpeted a new pact that nearly doubled the Korean broadcasting rights fees, the tour's largest revenue stream.

Clearly Bivens did a lot of things right, and I very enthusiastically believed in her leadership; the problem was not her vision but her interpersonal style. She is aggressive and confident, and people are terrified of a woman like that, especially within golf's old boys' network. She also didn't seem to make much of an effort to connect with the players, and many found her to be aloof and bulldoggish. Of course, none of that would have mattered if the tour was on solid footing, but with the schedule continuing to contract, the players were beginning to panic. After charting such an aggressive course, Bivens, according to numerous news reports, was reluctant to make concessions even as the economy imploded. Whether as a result of the budget concerns or Bivens, companies that had enjoyed long relationships with the LPGA started walking away. A blind item in one of the golf magazines quoted an unnamed executive who said he'd still like to sponsor an LPGA event but could no longer deal with "that woman." The remark echoed Bill Clinton's famous dis of Monica Lewinsky and highlighted some of the inherent sexism in the critiques of Bivens: Finchem is not exactly warm and cuddly, either, but he is celebrated as a hard-nosed businessman who gets results, not disparaged as a bitch.

All of this was a backdrop to the fateful dinner in Toledo. I have to admit I was miffed to have been excluded. Maybe that was because the other players knew that I was (and remain) a Bivens supporter. Maybe they simply didn't care what I thought—in golf, sometimes people are perceived to be only as smart as their place on the money list. Whatever the case, the Bivens situation was now my business because an emergency conference call among the player directors and the LPGA board was organized for Friday night at the Jamie Farr.

But first I had to play my second round, and it was a delight. Thanks in part to Donny's coaching, my putting continued to improve and that confidence seeped into the rest of my game. I played beautifully en route to a 68 that was my cleanest round in a month, making the cut easily as I moved up to forty-fifth place.

That night the conference call was convened. In 2009 the LPGA board was made up of seven players (president Michelle Ellis, VP Sherri Steinhauer, Helen Alfredsson, Pat Hurst, Juli

Inkster, Stacy Prammanasudh, and myself), the national president of the LPGA Teaching and Club Professionals, Patti Benson, and six independent directors plucked from the business world including Dawn Hudson, former president and CEO of Pepsi-Cola North America, and Nancy Wiese, former vice president of worldwide brand marketing for the Xerox Corporation. It's an impressive collection of brilliant businesspeople and veteran players experienced in the ways of the tour, and I was quite intimidated by their collective brainpower. To that point in my first term as a player director I had spent most of the time listening and learning. Friday night in Toledo, I finally found my voice. The tour is my life and I felt compelled to weigh in on the debate. These conversations are all confidential. I can't reveal what was said, but it was gratifying that my opinion mattered. Nothing was decided that night because it felt as if we had a little time to sort things out; word of the players' discontent had not yet gone public.

On Saturday it was back to golf as usual. My third round at the Farr was blighted by a bogey on the second hole but I responded with a nice little rally, birdying five, seven, and eight to begin sneaking up the leaderboard. The par-4 ninth hole was playing dead into the wind and my drive didn't go far enough to run down the hill in the landing area. I was left with an awkward downhill, sidehill lie. The ensuing approach shot came in too hot and rolled off the back of the green into a nasty patch of rough. A so-so chip left me thirty-five feet from the hole and I three-putted from there for a depressing double bogey. I never regained the momentum, ultimately signing for a 72 that dropped me to sixty-eighth place. I had stopped my missed-cut streak but was destined for another mediocre finish. The only positive was that after the round Nancy Lopez, the Hall of Famer who was my Solheim Cup captain in 2005, spent forty-five minutes coaching me on my putting on the practice green. She helped me pick out a new putter, an Odyssey Sabertooth, because she felt as though it helped me line up with the face more square. Nancy also introduced me to one of her favorite drills, sinking fifty five-footers in a row from all different angles around the hole. It took me forever to finish the drill, but by the time I walked off the practice green I felt a lot more confident with my putting.

On Sunday I rolled the ball quite nicely during a 69 that moved me up to fifty-fourth, worth $3,874. That afternoon, golf.com broke the news of the dinner mutiny. The U.S. Women's Open was up next. It's the most important tournament of the year, but the Bivens drama was now destined to be a big part of the story.

Following the final round of the Jamie Farr I caught a short flight to Newark, New Jersey, and then rented a car and made the quick drive to Bethlehem, Pennsylvania, the Open's host city. (To save money, some girls drove the five hundred miles from Toledo.) That night there was another conference call about Bivens, the beginning of an end-of-the-day ritual that was repeated on Monday, Tuesday, and Thursday. The calls sometimes lasted for upward of two hours, which was not the ideal way to prepare for our national championship. All that time on the phone definitely took an emotional toll on the player directors, but we had to do what we had to do. The first reports about the Toledo dinner had set off a feeding frenzy among all the media gathered at the Open. The commissioner went into hiding while her fate was decided, and at some point during the week it became clear that the situation was irreconcilable.

It was very poignant for me when word circulated among the board that Bivens had decided to resign. I enjoyed getting to know her during my stint as a player director and I felt sorry for her on a personal level. There was also a larger concern about the LPGA. The tour was already in such a precarious position, and the last thing we needed was more tumult. But I was very supportive of the board's decision to install one of its directors, Marsha J. Evans, as acting commissioner to get us through the rest of the season and to try to salvage the 2010 schedule. Marty is whip smart and very personable with a remarkable résumé: During her three decades serving her country, she became the first woman to command a U.S. naval station and rose to the rank of rear admiral, and, after retiring from the navy, she ran the Girl Scouts of America and then the American Red Cross.

Because of all the off-course distractions I think I was hyperfocused for my first round of the Open, as it was a relief to concentrate on golf and nothing else. The Old Course at Saucon Valley Country Club is a superb test, long and tough with beautiful bunkering and very challenging green complexes. The Open always has a great atmosphere but this was a cut above, as the galleries were big and boisterous and everyone associated with the tournament treated the players

Morgan Pressel (left), Paula Creamer, and I at the pro-am party in Singapore. Still think LPGA players aren't glamorous?

Having a shot at winning the Kraft Nabisco Championship got my year off to a rousing start. (ROBERT BECK/*SPORTS ILLUSTRATED*/GETTY IMAGES)

My elephant ride in Thailand was one of the most thrilling things I've ever done. This job is an adventure and you have to embrace it.

Backstage with Jason Mraz, one of my favorite singers. Before he signed my cleavage.

Michelle Wie and I taking the plunge during the week of the Evian Masters. It was cool watching Michelle grow up this year, on and off the golf course.

Yani Tseng (right), Meaghan Francella, and I at Morgan Pressel's twenty-first birthday party. Meaghan and I had a sloppy night, but Yani went out the next day and won the Corning Classic.

At Wet 'N Wild in Orlando with my boys Jan Meierling (right), Doug Parra (center), and Thomas Kogler (left). All the screaming and g-forces from the rides contributed to a lesion on my eyeball that would mess me up at the Evian Masters.

My working vacation at the Ladies Italian Open was a blast. Amid all the scrumptious meals, high-end shopping excursions, and jaw-dropping sightseeing, I found just enough time to make three eagles en route to a solid eleventh-place finish.

With Jennifer Rosales (center) and Dorothy Delasin for what constitutes a wild night out in Rochester, New York.

Michelle and I whooping it up during a four-ball victory at the 2009 Solheim Cup. She played supernatural golf that day, birdying six of the first eleven holes. (DARREN CARROLL/*SPORTS ILLUSTRATED*/GETTY IMAGES)

My old friend Natalie Gulbis and I continued our successful partnership from the 2005 Solheim Cup, winning a key foursomes match. (DARREN CARROLL/*SPORTS ILLUSTRATED*/GETTY IMAGES)

t meant a lot to me to share the Solheim triumph with my father, Man Kim, a Korean immigrant who is testament to America's wondrous melting pot. (DARREN CARROLL/*SPORTS ILLUSTRATED*/GETTY IMAGES)

This is the most emotional moment of my career so far: my dad wrapping me in a hug after I won my firs
tournament, in 2004. Given all I've gone through since, I think my next victory will be even more meaningful
(STEVE GRAYSON/WIREIMAGE.COM)

like goddesses. I felt good vibes even before I birdied my first hole of the championship (number ten, as I began on the back nine). Had I played the next seventy-one holes in even par I would have won by one stroke but, alas, it's not quite that easy. The eleventh is a brutal par-3 and I missed the green and made bogey. After that I settled into the round nicely with six straight pars, but then I got stuck on the bogey train, making three in a row beginning at eighteen. In that stretch I didn't hit any truly bad shots, but at the Open there is zero margin for error. I was three over par but I kept fighting, and at the par-3 fourth hole I played a sweet 6-iron to eight feet. Donny and I really grinded on reading the birdie putt—at one point he crouched down be-hind me, which no other caddie has ever done besides my dad. I poured in the putt, eliciting a fist pump from Donny. At the par-4 sixth hole I hit a perfect 6-iron to six feet for another birdie. My hard-fought one-over-par 72 left me in twelfth place.

The start to my second round was like CliffsNotes to my en-tire year: eagle, double bogey, double bogey. On the par-5 first hole I laid up to ninety-two yards and then for the second week in a row jarred a wedge shot, this one being my fourth eagle of the season. That shot me to fourth place on the leaderboard and set off a round of lusty high fives and hugs with Donny and the rest of my group. I was still a little too amped up on the next tee and overswung a bit, popping up my drive and leaving a very long approach into the green. My hybrid found the green-side bunker and I hit a miserable sand shot, leaving it in the bunker. There is nothing more embarrassing for a pro golfer, and my ears were burning as I heard the murmuring of the crowd. The ensuing double bogey was deflating, but I know freaky things happen at the U.S. Open so I tried to shrug it off. My double at the par-4 third hole was plain bad luck. I missed the fairway by about a foot and wound up in a gnarly patch of rough, forcing me to hack back into the fairway. From 101 yards I hit what I thought was a perfect wedge to a back pin, but my ball took a big, hard hop and bounced over the green. With the putting surface plunging away from me, the best I could do was pop it out to forty feet and two-putt. Just like that, I tumbled back into the middle of the pack.

I never regained my juju and struggled the rest of the way, failing to make a birdie. Still, one sequence on the fourteenth hole still gave me a big shot of confidence. I pulled my drive into the water, with the ball crossing the hazard line about 140 yards from the green. I was about to take a drop at the point of entry when Donny called me off. Per rule 21-6(b), I was allowed to take the penalty drop anywhere between where I struck my tee shot and the point of entry to the hazard. Donny had found a spot forty yards back from where he thought I could smoke a hybrid over the trees onto the green. I wasn't so sure, but he talked me into it and I hit a beautiful shot that nearly hit the flagstick before trickling twenty feet past.

"Great fucking shot!" Donny yelled. (Luckily, no rabbit-eared LPGA officials heard him.)

With a laugh, I said, "Between the two of us, only one person thought I could pull that off, and it wasn't me." Donny thinks I'm a better player than I do, which floored me.

My 76 left me in thirty-seventh place. I would've been more bummed about sliding down the leaderboard but for my dinner treat: Meg Mallon's nephew Dan. After our big night getting reacquainted at the LPGA Championship, we had been keeping in touch with phone calls and very flirtatious text messages. I was so excited to see him again, though our dinner was not unchaperoned, as Dan's aunt Meg tagged along, as did her friends Beth Daniel and Kelly Robbins. (Combined, those three chicks have a mind-blowing sixty career LPGA victories.) We all shared a fun, laughter-filled dinner, and Dan and I sneaked off afterward for some alone time, during which we finally had our first kiss. It was dreamy and romantic, not the sloppy, hormonal sucking of face you might expect after four years of buildup. Dan had to get back to his home in Pennsylvania the next day so we parted ways, but not before he said he wanted to take things slow. I wasn't really sure if that meant he liked me a lot and didn't want to mess this up, or if it was his way of politely blowing me off. There would be plenty of time to figure it out. That night I fell asleep with a smile on my face, and it had nothing to do with golf.

I needed a good third round to get back into the tournament, but it didn't happen. I played the front nine in one over par, and, arriving at the tee of the par-4 tenth, I was intrigued to discover that the tees had been moved up sixty yards, shortening the hole to about 285 yards in an effort to entice players into trying to drive the green. Seeing that I was stewing on whether or not to go for it, Donny offered a short piece of advice: "Go big or go home."

I unsheathed my driver but I wanted to hit a huge drive a little too much. My swing was way too fast and I jerked my ball into a fairway bunker. My second shot found another bunker and, after an indifferent third shot, I three-putted for a double bogey. That clinched it: I wasn't going to win the U.S. Open. I hacked my way to a back-nine 42 for a 79 that left me tied for sixty-first, ahead of exactly six players.

Sulking about my round afterward, I realized my mind had gotten way too cluttered when I was on the course: *Is my stance square? Is my left arm straight on the backswing? Is my downswing too steep? Are my hips too open when I'm putting? Is there too much weight on my left foot? Does Donny like me? Does my butt look big in this skirt?*

For the final round I decided to just turn off my brain and swing, freeing my mind from any thoughts about mechanics. After playing the front nine in one over, I birdied the tenth hole after a sweet approach shot. I almost did a cartwheel on the green—it had been an unfathomable forty-five holes since my last birdie. On fourteen I hit a gorgeous cut 6-iron to four feet for another birdie, and then on the short par-3 seventeenth I damn near made an ace, settling for a tap-in birdie. A textbook par on eighteen gave me a 71. Anytime you shoot even par in a U.S. Open it's a good feeling . . . even if it only moves you up to fifty-fourth place.

For my efforts I earned $10,736. (Eun-Hee Ji, a young Korean with maybe the sweetest swing on tour, banked $585,000 for her thrilling victory, which came by way of a twenty-five-footer for birdie on the seventy-second hole.) For the season I had now made $131,724. In the real world that's really good cheddar, but it left me a discouraging fifty-first on the money list. Money is not the only way to quantify performance. I hadn't earned a Solheim Cup point in three months and had slipped to eighth in the standings. There were two more tournaments left before the team was to be finalized: the Evian Masters in France and then the Women's British Open. The tour's annual European road trip figured to be even more eventful than usual.

CHAPTER 8

Euro-trashed

There was an off week before the Evian Masters so I enjoyed a little time at home in Orlando, practicing by day and hanging out with friends at night. My inner circle is mostly guys. Being out on tour is such a tacofest that when I'm home the last thing I want to do is be around more women. A typical night out involves dinner and a few drinks and just kind of hanging out. Most of my O-town friends are golfers because we seem to have more in common with each other than nine-to-five working stiffs. My BFF is Jan (pronounced *Yawn*) Meierling, a native of Germany who plays various minitours in the U.S. and Europe. During the dark week we spent a lot of time together on the golf course. Jan and I have pretty spirited matches, with the stakes usually being the loser has to buy the next meal. Occasionally we come up with racier bets. Playing a par-3 once, we had a closest-to-the-hole competition. If I lost I had to go to a famously rowdy strip club in Tampa, Mons Venus, and jump onstage with the girls. If Jan lost he would have to go to an adult novelty store and not only purchase an acorn-size butt plug but also ask the guy behind the counter for instructions on its use while I listened in via cell phone. I hit first and flagged my tee shot to ten feet. Jan was so rattled he skulled his shot over the green. He hasn't yet held up his end of the bargain, but he will. Trust me on that.

Part of hanging out with the boys means always being up for an adventure, so two days before I was to depart for the Evian Masters a group of us went to Wet 'N Wild, a water-slide amusement park. I had now lost thirty pounds in the three months since my journey to Korea so I decided to wear a two-piece bathing suit, which was a huge deal for me—I had never worn one in front of any non–family members, let alone four wolfish guys. I told them they were not allowed to look below my rib cage and we had a superfun day. Some of the waterslides are like liquid roller coasters, with big drops and all the corresponding screaming and crushing g-forces.

The next morning, July 17, I woke up and my right eye was feeling weird. You know when you look at the sun and for a few seconds afterward see spots? It was like that, but the spots wouldn't go away. Colors weren't quite right, either. For example, anything white looked a little bit copper. Naturally, I began freaking out and rushed to an optometrist. He diagnosed a tiny lesion on the back of my eyeball and pulled a few strings so I could be seen that afternoon by a retinal surgeon. The surgeon said it could take weeks, even months, for my eye to heal on its own, and my vision could be affected the whole time. I was devastated to hear this, so he laid out the only option that would not ruin my season: laser surgery. He could zap me right then and there, closing the lesion. If everything went smoothly, my vision would return to normal in seven to ten days. Of course I was freaked out by the prospect of messing with my eyes, but I know a lot of players who have had LASIK, and the surgeon assured me that the procedure he wanted to do was every bit as routine. After much cajoling, and a few teary phone calls to my mom and dad, I agreed to the laser surgery and we got busy. He numbed my eyeball with some drops of anesthetic that burned like a gallon of lemon juice. Then the surgeon zapped my poor little eyeball with a laser that harnesses the power of the sun, or so it seemed, because the heat and blinding light caused searing pain. Afterward I was told that everything had gone smoothly, but I was still pretty rattled.

Nevertheless, it was going to take a lot more than a funky eyeball to keep me from teeing it up across the pond, so that night I flew from Orlando to Newark and then caught a red-eye into Geneva. From there it's an hour's ride in a private car across the border into France, where the beautiful Alpine town of Évian-les-Bains awaits. For trips to Europe that begin with an overnight flight I always have a specific game plan to combat jet lag: sleep the first five hours, and then no more. It can be hard to pull off, but this schedule forces me to awaken about the same time the sun is rising over the Continent, getting my sleep cycle in sync for the rest of the trip. On this flight I wound up seated next to Dave Brooker, Lorena Ochoa's ex-caddie who, you may recall, was going to be my looper at the U.S. Women's Open before he jilted me for Suzann Pettersen. Dave is an old friend and we quickly became engrossed in conversation. Before I knew it, we were most of the way across the Atlantic and I hadn't slept a wink. Despite my best intentions, I crashed for the final two or three hours of the flight and it was days before I could get over the resulting jet lag.

The Evian Masters is one of the really special tournaments on the schedule, and not just because it offers the biggest purse of the year ($3.25 million). There is just something magical about the whole week, with the picturesque setting in the mountains, the charming villages to explore, the great French food. The Evian used to have extra meaning for me because it was where Mark and I had our first date in 2006 and where, in the ensuing two years, we enjoyed romantic anniversary celebrations. But enough about that.

For the tournament, most of the players stayed at the same swank resort. Following a practice round, I spent a long afternoon at the hotel pool with Michelle Wie and Morgan Pressel. We were doing goofy dives and taking underwater pictures and generally acting like unchaperoned teenyboppers, which, in fact, Michelle was. I wore a two-piece bathing suit again and even posted a few pictures on Twitter for the world to see.

Despite the fun times at the pool, I was beginning to get more and more stressed out as the week wore on. I kept thinking about the Solheim Cup points race, calculating and recalculating what I needed to do to stay in the top ten and how the girls farther down the points list could bump me off the team. With everything being so expensive in France, it also hit me how much I needed to make a good check. And the continuing problems with my eye certainly didn't help my state of mind.

By the start of the first round, my vision had improved but I was still seeing a tiny spot and a little discoloration. On the greens it was difficult to gauge all the contours correctly, and in general my depth perception was a little bit off. This was especially problematic because the Evian Masters Golf Club is basically built on the side of the mountain, with a lot of elevation changes and semiblind shots. It's already a challenging venue because at two thousand feet above sea level, the ball flies farther in the thin mountain air and you have to be very committed to the shot you're playing. Donny spent a lot of time during the practice rounds whispering in my ear about trusting the yardages, but it's hard to have complete faith when your eyes and your caddie are telling you different things.

The par-3 second hole is 160 yards on the scorecard, but it's so steeply downhill it plays as about a 125-yard shot. During the first round there was a light crosswind. I was in between clubs and went with a 9-iron but didn't swing it with conviction, catching the ball heavy. My tee shot finished well short of the green, and from there I chipped ten feet past the hole. For pace-of-play reasons, it is ordained that once all the players reach the green, the following group on the tee is waved up to hit their shots. So I had to stand around for ten minutes fretting about my par putt. I was so antsy that when it was finally my turn to putt, I wound up blasting my ball four feet past the hole. Then I misread the comebacker, missing badly and taking a brutal double bogey. On number four I misjudged my approach shot, coming up way short, and then couldn't get up and down. At the fifth hole I had an eighty-five-foot birdie putt that only went about sixty-five feet. I missed the par putt and just like that was four over through five holes. Walking off the green, I shed a tear or two. I was like, Is this really happening? With the week off and then the long journey to France, there was such a buildup to the tournament; then, in the space of a little more than an hour, I had pretty much ruined my week. I rallied with a birdie on the sixth hole and played even par the rest of the way for a 75 that left me in a thirteen-way tie for seventy-fifth place. That doesn't sound too horrible except that there were only ninety girls in the field.

My ball striking was crisper for the second round but I was still having trouble reading the greens, leading to a missed five-footer for birdie on number seven and a three-putt bogey on eight. Through fourteen holes I had three birdies and three bogeys, leaving me three over for the tournament, the projected cut line. Missing the cut is always a bummer, but it's particularly mortifying to do it at the Evian, where it's such a small field that the top seventy and ties still move on, leaving only a handful of losers idle on the weekend. A bad 9-iron on the fifteenth hole led to a bogey, so playing the sixteenth I was feeling a ton of pressure to make birdie.

I hit a good drive and had ninety-four yards to the flag, a perfect yardage for my 54-degree wedge. I felt good over the ball, but then, well, I'm not exactly sure what happened. All I know is that I hit a dead shank, my ball dribbling straight right into a grove of trees at a 90-degree angle from where I was aiming. As confirmation of the shank my ball even left a smudge on the club's hosel, like the mark of the beast on a sinner's forehead. I was so shocked I could barely exhale. Donny just picked up the bag and walked away, avoiding eye contact. The shank is the most feared shot in golf. It is not merely bad execution or a bad result. It is a total, complete breakdown, a

shot so horrid and unexpected it induces an almost supernatural fear and loathing in golfers. I had never hit a shank before
in competition and was still in a state of disbelief as I hacked
out of the trees, pitched onto the green, and two-putted for
double bogey.

Walking to the seventeenth tee, I tried to forget about the
shank by telling myself that with a birdie-birdie finish I could
still get back to four over par and have a shot at making the cut.
The seventeenth is a short, downhill par-3 that for the second
round was playing only 101 yards. I should've used my 54-
degree wedge, but just thinking about holding that club again
gave me the shivers, so I went with a pitching wedge and tried
to hit a little knockdown shot. It was way too much stick and I
flew the green, leading to another bogey. I sleepwalked to a par
at eighteen and signed for a 76, leaving me at +7. I was one of
sixteen girls to miss the cut and was so embarrassed about it—
and the shank—that I hid out in my room for the rest of the
evening.

The next day I considered hitting a million range balls but
decided instead a break from the game might do me some
good, so I spent three or four hours poolside. I got so tan my
skin was one shade from eggplant. In the late afternoon I am-
bled over to the course, though not to hit balls. One of the
cool traditions at the Evian Masters is that the tournament
has a private beer garden for the players and caddies, and all
the suds are free. So much Heineken gets guzzled that week
(mostly by the caddies), it's a wonder the company is still in
business. This was one of the only times in my life I've gone to
an LPGA event in civilian clothes, so I made the most of the

EURO-TRASHED   131

opportunity, wearing tight jeans, high heels, and one of my many sardonic T-shirts. This one has a picture of a sofa bed and beneath it the words I PULL OUT.

I dressed a bit spiffier that night for the black-tie ball that is another memorable part of Evian week. It's easy to forget how hot LPGA golfers are until they slip out of their visors and boxy polos and capri pants. Naturally, Natalie Gulbis created a stir with a little minidress, but she wasn't even the most va-va-voom player there. That was Maria Verchenova, a Russian goddess who plays on the Ladies European Tour.

After the party none of my colleagues wanted to go out on the town because, unlike me, they had to get some rest for the final round. But the caddies are always ready to party, so I joined four of them for a costly excursion to a nearby casino. Gambling with foreign currency is always dangerous because it doesn't look real and thus hurts less when you lose it. Afterward we journeyed to a sweaty nightclub. We were out on the dance floor in a little group when suddenly this Moroccan dude was up on me, talking French and trying to grind. I just ignored him and stayed with my friends. Later, this same guy tried to dance with me again. He spoke a little English, so I politely told him that I was just going to hang out with my boys.

At four A.M. I was ready to go back to my room. A couple of my friends offered to escort me on the short walk to the hotel, but they were so drunk I wasn't sure they could make it that far. Anyway, this is France, what's to worry about, right? So I said my good-byes and left alone. I was maybe fifty steps out of the club when I heard two sets of footsteps pounding down the pavement. For a woman walking alone at night, that's a very startling sound. I turned around and coming at me were two men, one of whom was the Moroccan guy from the dance floor. He was like, "You no dance with me? Why not?" My heart started to race a bit but, trying to act composed, I just laughed off his remark. Then he tried to put his arm around me. I shrugged it off without really acknowledging him. Guys like that get off if you show them you're uncomfortable. He tried to put his arm around me again, and this time I slung it off. By now I could feel the adrenaline flooding my body. It's funny how heightened your senses are when you feel threatened. I became aware that the Moroccan dude's friend was jangling a key chain in his pocket, and that's when I noticed we were standing in front of a parking garage. I wheeled around and began marching back toward the club and the guy put his arm around me once again, this time trying to steer me toward the garage. I shoved him violently and yelled, "Fuck off!" and began jogging back toward the club, four-inch heels be damned. Thank God they didn't follow me. I was shaking when I got back inside the club. My guy friends were still there and when I told them what happened, they were ready to run outside to brawl. I talked them out of it but did insist on an escort back to my hotel.

Growing up you always see the after-school specials on TV but you never think something like this can happen to you. It was definitely a mistake to put myself in a vulnerable position, but I'm glad I kept my wits about me. The whole scary episode was a reminder that as a young woman traveling the world alone, a little more caution might not be a bad thing.

The next day I got a two-hour massage and tried to pretend that the whole disastrous trip to France had never happened.

That Sunday night I caught a quick flight into Manchester, England, and then took an endless bus ride to Lancashire, the site of the Women's British Open. The next day my makeover began, beginning with some new equipment. My game was in such doldrums I needed to try to shake things up, so I switched back to my old Titleist ball and reshafted my driver, going back to the Diamana Blue Board I had used earlier in the year. I also met up with my new caddie. Before Donny and I hooked up, he had committed to caddie for Ted Purdy at the PGA Championship at Hazeltine National Golf Club in Minnesota. I wasn't thrilled that he was deserting me, but I couldn't tell him to turn down a PGA Tour cameo. My fill-in caddie was an English bloke named Andy Dearden. We'd been friendly for years but had never worked together. Andy was taking time off to be with his pregnant wife and out of the blue contacted me through Facebook to ask if I knew of any bags that were available for the Open. He was thrilled when I offered mine.

Monday afternoon I took my first spin around Royal Lytham & St. Annes, and the best part of the round was having two fully functional eyes: My vision had returned to normal in the preceding twenty-four hours. Lytham is a classic English links course—relatively flat, pretty narrow fairways, smallish greens, tons of devilish pot bunkers. It has a great history, having hosted ten British Opens, with a roster of Hall of Fame champions that includes Bobby Jones (1926), Peter

Thomson ('55), Gary Player ('74), and Seve Ballesteros ('79 and '88). In more recent times Tom Lehman ('96) and David Duval (2001) prevailed there. This impressive pedigree helps illustrate why professional golfers obsess about the major championships. There are only four per year, and they are played on the best courses, and under the most exacting conditions. Whereas the average fan can't articulate the difference between the LPGA State Farm Classic and the Navistar LPGA Classic, everyone knows the importance of the Women's British Open, and that by winning it—or any of the other majors—a player writes herself into the history of the game. The self-imposed pressure to perform, along with the rigors of the courses, is what makes majors such grueling mental and physical tests and explains why, over time, only the very best players have emerged as champions.

I got to know Lytham when the Women's British was played there in 2003 and '06, and, frankly, I hated the place. That had more to do with my general distaste for links golf, in which the wind and brick-hard turf and blind shots and quirky layouts often result in good shots winding up in horrible places. I'm sure my bad attitude explains why I had finished better than twenty-eighth only once in six career Opens.

During our first practice round together, on Monday afternoon, Andy wondered if I was physically okay because I was hitting the ball so poorly.

"Are you tight?" he asked.

"I'm Asian, of course I'm tight. Take that any way you like."

In France I had bought two bottles of Montrachet wine for a friend back home. After my dinner plans fell through that night, I wound up getting fish and chips takeaway to eat on the bed in my hotel room and washed it down with an entire bottle of the Montrachet, all by my lonesome. Ah, the glamorous life of a professional golfer.

My mood was scarcely better the next day. Only on the LPGA Tour are there pro-ams during the week of major championships, during which the players have to endure long rounds alongside backslapping amateurs who have paid a princely sum for the experience. Because of my lowly position on the money list I wasn't in the pro-am and thus couldn't play the course until after it was over, at nearly four P.M. When Andy and I teed off it was raining and windy and miserable and I made a mess of the first two holes. On number three I popped up my drive and had a 5-iron left. What followed was an epiphany that dramatically changed the trajectory of my Open. During the off week prior to the Evian Masters, and then while I was in France, I spent all of my time working on and thinking about my fundamentals. I had become obsessed with my ball position and alignment and swing path and tempo. But standing in the third fairway of Royal Lytham's I just thought, Why am I trying to be perfect? I'm a funny-looking girl with a homemade swing, so why not just embrace it? Lorena Ochoa doesn't have a textbook swing. Neither does Nancy Lopez. Or, for that matter, Jim Furyk or Lee Trevino or so many other great players. Here I was playing the holy Open, on the sacred English linksland, with a salty English caddie in quintessential English weather and I was trying to be a perfect American robot making perfect swings. Golf is art, not science. It's about creating shots, not mindlessly repeating the same swing over and over. Right there in the third fairway, all of this raced through my mind. As I waggled my 5-iron I banished any thoughts about fundamentals and just visualized the low, stinging cut I wanted to play. Then I executed it beautifully, my ball rifling through the wind to within six feet of the flag. Were this a cheesy sports movie like *Rudy*, the camera would have swirled around me and captured my elegant follow-through and beatific smile as I watched the shot paint the sky.

For the first time in two days I had impressed Andy. "Fucking nice of you to finally join us," he harrumphed.

Suddenly my shoulders lifted and horrible things began coming out of my mouth and I felt like myself again. I played great during the Wednesday practice round and begrudgingly began to fall in love with the quirks of the course, which forced me to play with more imagination and panache. My equipment changes also helped my new commitment to playing by feel. I had put a couple of new hybrids in the bag during the U.S. Women's Open, so this was the first time I was using them with the Titleist Pro-V1x. Andy would be like, "How far do you hit this four-hybrid?"

"I don't know."

"What do you mean, 'I don't know'?"

"It doesn't matter, I can see the shot."

I had reached this blissful metaphysical state where I knew exactly what I wanted to do and just let my body do it. From, say, 152 yards there's a wide variety of different shots I can play: a low, hard, drawing 9-iron; a stock 8-iron; a high, soft, cut 7-iron; a choked down, bump-and-run 6-iron; and other more exotic plays depending on the wind and lie and my mood. At Lytham I simply picked one shot, visualized it in my head, committed to it, and let fly.

I was definitely helped by Andy's sage advice and our playful chemistry. He has caddied at numerous tournaments at Lytham and is familiar with every hump and hollow. At one point on Wednesday I told him, "You know this place like the back of your hand."

His reply: "More like the front of my palm." That became one of our mottos for the week.

Once the tournament proper began I was tested right from the start, with bogeys on the second and fourth holes. Instead of being overly discouraged I just told myself that Lytham is a tough course, the wind is blowing and bogeys are inevitable, so keep grinding. I reached the par-5 sixth hole in two shots but then three-putted for a par. Now I was pissed off. On the seventh tee I smashed a 350-yard drive (downwind!) and after that started swinging more aggressively. On the ninth hole I hit one of the purest 9-irons of my life to set up my first birdie of the round. For my second shot at the par-5 eleventh I played this awesome low, slinging 4-iron to twenty feet, leading to a two-putt birdie. As my confidence increased I started to really let loose with my driver, and suddenly I was hitting it as long as I did thirty pounds ago. On the long par-4 fourteenth I smoked a drive and followed with a 7-iron to the heart of the green. When my twenty-two-footer for birdie tumbled in, I did a big fist pump and let out a piercing "*Whooooo!*" Andy, English gent that he is, could only laugh and shake his head at me.

I felt like my one-over-par 73 was a pretty good result, but having teed off so early I didn't have a sense of how it stacked up versus the field. When I came off the course I checked the scoring computers and 73 left me around fortieth place, but as more scores trickled in I kept moving up. To thirty-fourth place. Then twenty-eighth. Then twenty-first . . . sixteenth . . . eleventh . . . and, finally, by day's end, a tie for seventh. I was thrilled to be back in contention at another major championship.

After resting in my hotel room for a bit, I returned late in the afternoon for a little practice. In my locker was a note from U.S. Solheim Cup captain Beth Daniel. It was short and sweet: "Christina, congratulations on making the team!" I guess Beth and her people had been running the numbers and, given my strong start, there was no way I could get bumped out of the top ten in the points race. Reading the note I let out so many shrieks a clubhouse attendant rushed over to make sure I hadn't sliced off a finger with the locker door. Making the Solheim Cup team was my number-one goal for the season and it felt so uplifting to have achieved it. Much of the rest of the afternoon was spent whooping it up on the driving range with my soon-to-be teammates.

Floating to the first tee to begin my second round, I was still on such a high. For various logistical reasons Lytham was reconfigured for the Open, so our first hole was a par-3, a highly unusual way to start a round. My jolly mood evaporated when I yanked my tee shot way left and had to scramble for a bogey. I bogeyed the fourth hole for a second straight day but then settled down with four straight pars. At the par-3 ninth hole the wind had switched so I had to smash a 7-iron to reach the green. I poured in the eighteen-footer for a much-needed birdie. At the par-5 eleventh I uncorked a banana slice with my second shot but played a pretty good pitch out of the heather to within thirty-five feet of the flag. I wanted to make the putt so desperately and it looked good the whole way. I feared it might have a little too much pace to take the break so I began screaming at my ball, "Turn, turn, give it to me, *give it to me!*" And it did—birdie. A bogey at fourteen was offset by back-to-back birds on fifteen and sixteen, and they nicely illustrated how much of a factor wind is at the Open. At the fifteenth I was dead into the fan and had to murder a 9-iron from 110 yards. On sixteen the breeze was at my back so I hit a baby pitching wedge from 130 yards.

My 71 left me at even par for the tournament, tied for fifth, three back of leader Catriona Matthew, who had gone absolutely bonkers on the back nine. Beginning on the eleventh hole she went eagle, ace, birdie, par, birdie, birdie, bogey, birdie, coming home in 30 strokes for a 67. (For us Lytham's back nine was par 37, the front par 35.) Matthew is one of the best players ever to come out of Scotland so she always enjoys tremendous crowd support at the Open, but she was even more of a sentimental favorite this time around because she was only eleven weeks removed from having given birth to her second child. If that weren't enough, the week before in France there had been a fire in the hotel where she and her husband and caddie Graeme were staying. Without even stopping to put on their shoes, Catriona and Graeme ran down the hallway yelling "Fire!" and banging on doors to alert fellow guests including LPGA player Amy Yang and her dad. Their heroism was credited with saving lives. Poor Graeme's bare feet were burned badly enough that he was unable to caddie for Catriona at the Evian Masters. He was back on the bag at the Open and, understandably, there was a tremendous outpouring of support for both Matthews.

Following my 71, Jane Park and I decided to explore the nearby city of Blackpool, or, as the players call it, Cesspool. It's basically the Atlantic City of England—a tacky, touristy area that is a little rough around the edges. We had heard that riding donkeys on the beach is a local tradition but were crestfallen to discover that it's for kids only. We had to make do with another amusement, these giant plastic balls you step into and then bob around in atop the water of this little inlet near the beach. You basically have to run like a hamster to stay upright. Unfortunately, I'm a little—okay, a lot—topheavy and Jane is kind of back-heavy, so we could both barely stand up. It was hysterical fun, and a nice way to take my mind off the fact that I was now in prime position to win the Women's British Open.

For the third round I was paired with Yani Tseng. She's a really cool girl, but it's never fun to play with Yani because she's such an animal off the tee. I've always been one of the longer hitters on tour, but when Yani and I were paired together a couple months earlier at the Sybase Classic, when I was struggling with my driver, it was demoralizing to have her blow it thirty and forty yards past me all day. But now that I was swinging with more confidence and aggression I had closed most of that distance gap; this gave me a big shot of confidence during my very clean front nine, which featured a bummer three-putt bogey from fifty feet on the first hole and then eight straight pars.

There was a big wind blowing, and the pins were in tougher spots, so I knew it would be a war of attrition and therefore was more than happy to be piling up pars. On the par-5 eleventh hole I laid up to fifty-seven yards and then carved a stellar wedge shot through the wind, landing it eight paces past the hole and then spinning it back to four feet for my first birdie. On eighteen I roped a 285-yard drive and then hit a punched 7-iron stone dead for a fantastic finishing birdie. My 71 had shot me up to solo second place, three back of Matthew, who had played her final fourteen holes in three under to match my 71 and push the lead to −4. We were the only players under par for the tournament.

After my round I was taken to the press room. Jousting with the European writers is always interesting, and this was no exception. One of the chaps said, "The final twosome of you and Catriona is a bit like Laurel and Hardy." I induced a lot of laughter when I said, "I don't know that show, unfortunately." Catriona is definitely pretty reserved on the golf course, but she's a sweetheart and we've had fun playing together in the past. I knew the crowd would be pulling for her, as they should.

Arriving at the first tee for our one P.M. final-round pairing I made the pleasant discovery that when Brits bellow "Catriona!" the accent makes it sound exactly like "Christina!" So I felt like the thousands of fans were serenading me and I hammed it up for them, waving like the Queen Mum. I was surprisingly re-laxed, perhaps owing to my mellow morning. When I got out of bed I fired up my Kindle and dived back into *Tantra for Erotic Empowerment: The Key to Enriching Your Erotic Life*. Of late I had been doing a lot of reading about Buddhism, Taoism, and other mind-altering subjects, and this Tantra book was quite engrossing, as you might imagine.

For the final round the first hole was playing a full-blooded 198 yards, but I was so jazzed I went with a 5-iron. I smoked it, a perfect draw that wound up eight feet from the flag. Catriona pulled her tee shot way left into the crowd and had to scramble for a bogey. I could have cut the lead to one stroke right then, but I misread my putt and settled for par.

On the par-4 second I was 185 yards from the hole. Throughout the week I had become adept at using the contours of the ground to shape shots. (In the U.S., most courses are so overwatered and overfertilized that the ball just stops dead upon landing, but the drier, firmer linksland terrain lets the ball bounce and run.) I landed my hybrid shot on the front of the green, as planned, but it took an unexpectedly soft bounce and stopped forty-five feet short of the hole. That was frustrating. Even worse was leaving my birdie putt five feet short and then missing that one for a bad bogey.

When Catriona bogeyed the third hole I was again within two of the lead, but I gave another shot back at number four when I sliced my 3-wood off the tee into a horrible bit of rough. I tried to reach the green but couldn't muscle it that far, and a so-so pitch led to a bogey. At this point I was not a happy kitty. I was making the kind of mistakes I had avoided over the first three rounds. I had a long talk with myself on the tee of the par-3 fifth hole and followed with what I thought was a perfect 8-iron. But my ball landed about one foot short of the crest of a mound on the front of the green and stopped abruptly. Had my unfaithful Titleist flown just a tiny bit farther, it would have funneled down the sloping green all the way to the flag for an easy birdie try. Now I was facing a brutally fast fifty-foot putt. Sometimes this really is a game of inches. Afraid of the speed of the putt, I left my birdie try eight feet short, leaving me with a knee knocker to save par. I'm not gonna lie: I was feeling a lot of pressure over the putt and I made a hurried stroke, missing badly. Bogey. Again. I was now four strokes off Catriona's lead and free-falling down the leaderboard into a tie for fourth place.

Walking off the fifth green I had tears welling up in my eyes. Just then I got some much-needed inspiration from my biggest fan, a lovely thirteen-year-old local named Jesica. She had followed me throughout the first round, and between every green and tee she was there to offer a smile or some bubbly words of encouragement. Afterward I signed some autographs for Jesica and we chitchatted about her own aspirations of playing professionally. She followed me for every ensuing hole and I was so touched by her devotion that Saturday evening I gave her the hat I had worn during the round; we also exchanged e-mails so we could keep in touch. So now, after my bogey on the fifth hole on Sunday, I was walking toward the next tee when Jesica's chirpy voice rang out. "You can do this, Christina!" she yelled, and hearing that gave me the little jolt of energy I needed. I made a very solid par on number six to stop the bleeding.

The par-5 seventh hole is where my comeback began. I had learned a very valuable lesson three months earlier during the tough final round of the Kraft Nabisco Championship, when I failed to make a birdie over the final fifteen holes: The only way to combat the pressure of a major championship Sunday is to play aggressively. The natural tendency is to be cautious and try to avoid mistakes, but that's not how you win tournaments. As I stepped to the seventh tee at Lytham I kept telling myself to be fearless, and it finally paid off. I ripped a 285-yard drive and then followed with a balls-out 3-wood to reach the green, setting up a crucial two-putt birdie. When Catriona bogeyed the tenth hole I was again within two strokes of her lead.

All week my game plan on the nasty little par-3 twelfth had been to play for the center of the green, regardless of the hole location. This time I aimed right at the flag. I made one of my best swings of the summer, sticking my tee shot to within a foot of the hole. It was a great scene—the crowd was going crazy, and so was I. Walking to the green I felt so proud of myself. After the ragged start I could have easily packed it in, but I kept fighting, and now, after brushing in the birdie putt, I was back to within one stroke of Catriona, who was struggling mightily. I really thought I was going to win the Open, and I felt okay with it. I wasn't the least bit intimidated by the opportunity.

The thing about golf is that you can't play defense against your opponents. Suddenly Catriona found her game and there was nothing I could do to cool her off. She hit a great shot into the thirteenth green to make her first birdie of the day and push the lead to two strokes. I thought I might get it all back on fourteen. Catriona drove it way left into the weeds while I was in the center of the fairway. But she followed with an incredible low, running shot that skirted around a bunker onto the green, about thirty feet from the hole. I generally try not to pay attention to what my opponent is doing, but I couldn't help but be impressed by that play. It was definitely a big momentum shift, and I got caught up trying to match Catriona's heroics. I rushed my swing and wound up shoving my approach shot right of the green. A pretty good pitch left me eight feet for par. As I was eyeing my putt, Catriona stepped up and holed her long putt for an impossible birdie. That was like a punch to the solar plexus. After our drives, I thought we might be tied walking off this green. Now I had a testy eight-footer just to stay within three strokes. I was so concerned with how much the putt meant, I failed to lose myself in the process of making a good stroke. I missed, taking a devastating bogey. I was now four strokes back with four holes to play. Game over.

Catriona went on to birdie the next hole, too. (So did I, not that it mattered.) Three birdies in a row in the middle of the back nine on Sunday at a major is pretty macho, and she definitely deserved to win. In the scoring trailer after the round I gave her a long hug and was genuinely so happy for her. The baby, the fire, her mind-blowing back nine on Friday . . . it just seemed predestined that Catriona would win.

Naturally I was a little bummed not to have prevailed, but I took nothing but positives from this near miss. When I arrived in England, my swing and my eye were a mess and I was stressing about money and Solheim Cup points. I was leaving Lytham with a ton of confidence and a new outlook on how to play the game, not to mention $109,500. (The check for my third-place tie shot me from fifty-fourth to forty-second on the money list.) The Women's British Open is a great tournament, don't get me wrong, but the only people who were truly disappointed I didn't win were my family, the coauthor of this book, and maybe a few Twitter followers. Now I was headed to the Solheim Cup, where there's so much more at stake. I would be playing for my captain, my teammates and, oh, about 305 million fellow Americans.

CHAPTER 9

"U-S-A! K-I-M!"

The Solheim Cup is women's golf's answer to the Ryder Cup, a goodwill match/blood feud pitting the U.S. versus Europe every other year. This Solheim had extra meaning for me because it was four years in the making.

I had qualified for the team in 2005, and it was one of the greatest weeks of my life. I played really well, going 2–1–1 in the match-play format, and all of my usual emoting was a big hit with the home crowd at Crooked Stick Golf Club in Carmel, Indiana. *GolfWorld* put me on the cover doing a zany fist pump with the headline LOUD AND PROUD. The confidence I gained that week definitely helped my golf game, but more important was how much I grew as a person. Back in '05, I was still traveling with my mom and dad full-time. I was friendly with my fellow players but not really friends with any of them. The Solheim Cup freed me—I got to know the other girls on such a deep level, and the relationships that were formed that week helped liberate me from my parents.

Probably the biggest breakthrough came with Paula Creamer. Things had always been a little awkward between us. We grew up competing against each other in Northern California—she beat me in a tense play-off when she was twelve and I was fifteen, and that was the start of it. If I'm honest, a lot of the strain was jealousy on my part because she was younger and better and blonder than me. I had been the youngest one to win a number of regional tournaments and then Paula came along and broke all of my records, and looked so cute while doing it. At the Solheim we both finally let down our guards and realized how much we have in common and how much we enjoy being around each other. Paula is definitely the all-American girl and she's as sweet as pie, but she also possesses a very dry sense of humor. If trash-talking commences, some of her comebacks are lethal. She's one of my girls, and it all started because we were thrown together as teammates.

The Solheim Cup is like a drug—all it takes is one taste and you're hooked, maybe because of all the adrenaline and endorphins that are released while playing under such extreme pressure. Because of my great rookie experience I was obsessed with making the team in 2007, and all the extra stress had a negative effect on my game. There is a two-year running points race to determine the ten players who automatically qualify for the team. I finished fourteenth but was confident I had impressed captain Betsy King enough to warrant one of her two captain's choices. In the three months before the teams were finalized I had been kicking butt with four top-ten finishes, including a tie for second at the Safeway Classic, the final event in the qualifying period. Betsy was going to announce her picks at the conclusion of the Safeway, and I played my heart out knowing it was my last chance to impress her. Nearly winning had to clinch my spot on the team, right? I was euphoric after my stellar final round. Bounding into the locker room I bumped into Betsy, who had gathered her ten automatic qualifiers for the press conference to announce the captain's picks. Seeing me float in, Betsy put her arm around my shoulder and said, "Christina, I am so, so sorry." Being the silliest person in the world, I thought she was kidding. A little laugh even gurgled out of me. But then I could see in her face she was dead serious. (Moments later, Betsy would announce as her picks two players who finished ahead of me on the points list, Laura Diaz and Nicole Castrale.) All of the life drained out of my body and the only thing I could manage to squeak was, "Really?" I felt so stupid, not to mention crushed. After taking a few moments to compose myself, I thanked Betsy for considering me and then said, "I'm gonna go cry now."

I walked to a distant corner of the locker room, collapsed onto the floor, and started bawling so hard I thought my lungs were going to come out of my mouth. The other players found me on the floor and kind of piled on top in one big sloppy group hug. Everybody was crying like it was the first time they were watching *Titanic*. It was one of the worst days of my life; all the drama surrounding my failure to make the team I now refer to simply as the Tragedy of 2007. So at the '09 Solheim I would be seeking to earn points for my team, as well as some overdue validation.

After the Women's British Open ended on August 2, I flew directly into Chicago for three days of practice with my Solheim teammates at the host venue, Rich Harvest Farms, a very private facility built among the cornfields about sixty miles west of the downtown, in the hamlet of Sugar Grove. From there I journeyed to Virginia Beach, Virginia, to see Meg Mallon's nephew Dan. He had been, in his words, "cyberstalking" me while I was overseas. I thought this quick visit would be a good way to take my mind off the Solheim Cup pressure, and I was excited to see where things were going with Dan. He and his family had gathered for a family vacation, and with all of his aunts and uncles and nieces and nephews there were nineteen people staying in one ginormous house on the beach. I had lots of fun with his family but was a little freaked out by how nice and normal and nondysfunctional they were. I'm definitely not used to that. I only spent about twenty-four hours there, but upon arriving back home in Orlando, I received a text from Dan saying that everyone really liked me and his little nieces and nephews had been especially charmed. This left me with an unfamiliar warm and fuzzy feeling.

I spent the next six days at home working on my game, focusing on the natural, instinctive style of play that suited me so well at the Women's British Open. Before arriving at the Solheim Cup, I made a side trip to New York City for Cristie Kerr's annual Birdies for Breast Cancer fundraiser. Cristie founded the event in 2003 after her mother was diagnosed with the disease, and it has become a very impressive operation. The 2009 event would raise more than $350,000, meaning in seven years B4BC has contributed more than one million dollars to the Susan G. Komen for the Cure foundation. I told myself I would play the event to keep my game in shape but, as usual, I wound up getting a little distracted.

After getting picked up in a white-on-white Rolls-Royce Phantom and dropped at the Ritz—thanks, Cristie!—I hooked up with my LPGA colleague Dorothy Delasin and we went out on the town, first to a swank restaurant in SoHo and then to a lively lounge where a friend of a friend was bartending. At two thirty A.M. we wound up at a rooftop party and I didn't get to my room until almost four. But I was fine for the next morning's pro-am because I didn't drink much—recently I had decided that alcohol was a waste of money, and, anyway, I'm bad enough sober.

My pro-am pairing was spectacular, three former hockey teammates of Cristie's husband. They were the coolest guys, and all three just happened to be very good-looking. (What is it about hockey players, anyway?) On the sixteenth hole at Liberty National Golf Course—Cristie's home course—my playing partner, Jason, was sizing up a chip for eagle when his buddy said he'd jump in the lake if Jason holed it. He did. Splash. I almost hyperventilated, I was laughing so hard. That night Jason and I went barhopping in Manhattan's Meatpacking District. It was a blast and I didn't get back to my room until five A.M. I slept in the next day and then flew to Chicago for the Solheim Cup, a bit worn out and with my voice shot, but otherwise ready to rumble.

At Rich Harvest Farms the players were housed on-site in a cluster of cottages, each with four bedrooms that opened up to a common living room. I was rooming with Natalie Gulbis, Angela Stanford, and Brittany Lang. When I sprinted into our cottage, every inch was decked out in red, white, and blue—toilet-seat covers, bath mats, stickers on the windows, you name it. I began squealing like it was Christmas morning. By Sunday evening the whole team had arrived and it was absolute mayhem. The Solheim marries the intensity and sense of purpose of going into battle with the giggly, goofy fun of sleepaway camp. Pro golfers usually lead solitary lives, but the Solheim is an intensely communal experience. The team is cloistered away from the outside world, and only significant others are allowed into our little bubble—no parents or agents or swing coaches or any other entourage members. So we eat every meal together, practice together, and stay up late at night gabbing together. Some of the emotion that pours out is unforgettable. At one dinner, Juli Inkster got up to say a few words. She was forty-nine years old, so this was likely the last go-around for one of the greatest Solheim Cup players of all time. "I remember it wasn't that long ago the media was saying how old the U.S. Solheim Cup team is and wondering where all the good young American golfers are," Juli said. "Now look around this room. You truly embody what this event is all about, with your youth and talent and energy and camaraderie. I am so damn proud and honored to be a part of this team."

At this point Juli choked up. She might be the most cutthroat competitor on tour, and none of us had ever seen her cry before. Pretty soon everyone in the room was blinking back tears, too. The friendships that are forged at the Solheim have nothing to do with the golf, really. It's about tearing our hearts open and learning so much about each other.

At the same time, we had so much star power on our team I came in wondering if anybody's ego would get in the way. But from the very beginning there was no hierarchy, just twelve equals working toward one common goal. One of the most interesting developments of the week was watching Michelle Wie blossom in this warm, nurturing environment. She was kind of like me circa 2005, still searching for her niche on tour. On the course, her rookie year had already been a success, with seven top-fifteen finishes to that point—impressive enough to warrant one of Beth Daniel's captain's picks. The media is predisposed to pick on Michelle, but there was almost no second-guessing of Captain Daniel because at the time of her selection Michelle led the tour in birdie average and was in the top five in driving distance, making her potentially potent in match play. We all knew Michelle belonged, and she effortlessly integrated herself into the team. On tour Michelle has a small, tight clique of friends, but from the second she arrived at the Solheim she was so confident and free, walking up to every teammate and starting conversations. She was in the middle of all the late-night talks about life and golf and boys. Everyone was so charmed to discover what I already knew, that Michelle is just a really sweet, down-to-earth free spirit.

After four days of practice rounds, the team gathered for dinner on the eve of the opening session of four better-ball matches. It was pretty rowdy until Beth Daniel walked in, and then a hush fell over the room. She was holding a paper with the pairings, and in the loud, deep voice of the master of ceremonies at a wrestling extravaganza, she bellowed, "First up, Paula Creamer and Cristie Kerr . . ." The room exploded, and it only got louder as each team was announced. With four two-woman teams going out in the morning session, that meant four American players would be sitting out, and when Beth yelled out our final pairing, a little pang of disappointment ran through me, like,

Dang, I'm benched even though I've been playing so well in practice.
But I quickly reminded myself to get over it because the Solheim
Cup is not about any one individual. Then Beth took me aside
and said she was saving me for the afternoon session, when I
would be sent out first. "I need you to bring home a point, and I
need you to fire up the crowd," she said, and suddenly I felt so
important, like I was a key part of a larger plan. That night I had
trouble falling asleep because I was so pumped up.

The Solheim Cup features a match-play format that is unlike
any other event we play. Each hole is a tournament within a
tournament; you either win, lose, or halve a hole, and that is
how the score is kept, not with strokes. (Win the first hole and
you're "1 up." Take the second hole and you're "2 up." A match
that ends "3 & 2" means one team is three holes up with only
two left to play.) Across the Solheim's three days there are a total of twenty-eight matches, each worth one point. Since the
U.S. won the Cup in 2007, we needed only 14 points to retain
it. The Euros needed 14½ points to wrest the trophy away.
(For matches that are tied after eighteen holes, each team re-
ceives half a point.)

The U.S. team got off to a fast start in the morning session,
taking a 2½–1½ point lead. I was at the range warming up for
my afternoon alternate-shot match when assistant captain Meg
Mallon screeched up in a golf cart. "I have a gift for you!" she
yelled, and her nephew Dan popped out of the cart. I knew he
was coming, but wasn't sure when he would arrive. Naturally, I
was thrilled to see Dan and I gave him a big hug. But I had to get
my game face on, so I said, "I'm so happy you're here! And now
I have to pretend like you no longer exist."

About ten minutes before our tee time, my partner Natalie

Gulbis walked to the first tee, as did our opponents, the power-house Nordic duo of Suzann Pettersen and Sophie Gustafson. I lingered on the range a couple hundred feet away, listening to the crowd in the massive grandstand chant, "U-S-A! U-S-A!" I don't like to stand on the first tee at any tournament for too long because I get antsy, and here at the Solheim I had been jumping out of my skin since breakfast. Finally, a minute or two before we were supposed to tee off, I jogged onto the tee and the gallery went nuts.

The alternate-shot format we were playing forces each team to do a little strategizing. Natalie wanted me to tee off on the odd-numbered holes. I hit the ball farther than she does, and the way Rich Harvest Farms was sequenced, a lot of the longest holes happened to be odd-numbered. This worked out well because I wanted Natalie to have the birdie putts on the even holes since they featured some of the trickiest greens, and she's one of the two or three best putters on tour. Any opening tee shot at the Solheim Cup is intimidating, but I managed to smash a good drive down the right side of the fairway. Natalie followed with a gorgeous 7-iron to three feet, leading to a deafening roar from the gallery. I was left with a tough little putt, a downhill left-to-right slider with a lot of break. But I didn't feel nervous, just determined to come through for my partner. All I could think was, *No way I'm gonna let this girl down after that shot.* I drilled the birdie putt to put us 1 up.

On the par-5 second hole, Natalie hit a good drive and I decided to go for a green that's guarded by water. I caught my 3-wood thin and it screamed toward the lake. But this miraculous Jesus ball skipped twice on the water and rolled all the way into a greenside bunker. In my career I've only had a couple of balls walk on water like that. It was such a lucky break I was laughing my tits off. Natalie followed with a good bunker shot, leaving me with an uphill twelve-footer for birdie.

"Sorry I didn't hit it closer, partner," she said.

"That's okay, I got this," I replied. I never had a doubt I would make the putt, and I did. Two up.

The Euros won the fourth hole but I got it back on the par-4 sixth hole when I hit a 9-iron to a foot. The fans were going out of their minds and I yelled to Natalie, "I'm having the best time of my life!" We had been Solheim partners in 2005, getting a crucial victory in the first match of day two, which began with the U.S. trailing 5–3. Natalie and I enjoyed such great chemistry that day probably because we've been friends for so long. We first met at a Junior Golf Association of Northern California tournament when I was twelve and she was thirteen. All these years later I remember the details precisely. I had just shot 89 and was standing in front of a large scoreboard when Natalie materialized next to me. She was like five foot seven and already a knockout. Someone asked her how she played and she said, "Not so great, I shot seventy-six." As a nascent golfer I couldn't even conceive of a score that low and I was absolutely awestruck by this girl. At that moment I really believed she was the best golfer on the planet. Six years later we had both made it to the LPGA, and the very first tournament of my rookie year, in Tucson, I was making a peanut-butter-and-jelly sandwich in the player dining area when Natalie came up and congratulated me on having reached the big leagues. "We're living the dream, aren't we?" she said with typical enthusiasm. That quote has always stayed with me and I try to remember it whenever I'm feeling down about life on tour. Now, walking toward the sixth green of Rich Harvest Farms to pocket my conceded birdie, Natalie said something else that touched me deeply: "We really, really missed you, Christina. We as a team need you so much."

We halved the next seven holes in the match and then on fourteen Natalie was so pumped up she drove it 285 yards with a 3-wood. I followed with a crisp pitching wedge to ten feet and she coolly rolled in the birdie putt to win the hole, putting us 3 up with four to play. We won the sixteenth hole, too, closing the books on a 4 & 2 ass whooping.

One of the coolest things about winning a Solheim match is that you then get to jump onto a golf cart and zoom around the course cheering on your teammates, and everywhere you go, a hero's welcome awaits. I just spooned up all the cheering and hugs and congratulations. I had been dreaming about this day for four years, and it was even sweeter than I could have imagined.

Dan joined me for the team dinner that night. I had to get Beth Daniel's okay—usually only husbands or longtime loves are allowed—but since I had played so well she figured Dan was a good-luck charm and gave her blessing. It was so fun to have him there, and he mixed very well with my teammates, a few of whom were all too happy to grill him about our budding relationship.

At one point in the evening I offered a toast to our rookies Michelle, Kristy McPherson ("K-Mac"), and Brittany Lang ("B-Lang"). "You just tore your Sol-hymens!" I said. "You're no longer Solheim virgins!"

When it came time to announce the next morning's pairings, the first names Beth called were Michelle Wie and . . . Christina Kim! Michelle and I jumped out of our chairs and started screaming and then dancing together. The entire Solheim week was set to a hip-hop beat. Weeks earlier, Beth had asked each of us to name a favorite song that gets us pumped up and she burned a CD for each player with the various tunes. Almost all of them were thumping rap anthems. Paula chose Savage & Soulja Boy's "Swing," while I went with Fabolous's "My Time." Every night after dinner someone would put the music on and we'd have dance-a-thons until the wee hours.

Michelle had played in the opening day's morning session, halving her match and along the way displaying more emotion than any of us had ever seen out of her. That intensity only increased in our match versus Helen Alfredsson, the wily forty-four-year-old who had captained Europe's team two years earlier, and her partner Tania Elosegui, a rookie out of Spain with an elegant game. On number one Helen chipped in for birdie to steal the hole. Michelle turned to me and said, "That's fine, that's what they're gonna have to do to win a hole." On the par-5 second Michelle and I had birdie putts but Tania knocked in a fifteen-footer for eagle to put us 2 down. Michelle dropped her ball for practice and brushed in her twelve-footer. "I would have made it anyway," she sniffed. Walking off the green, she added, "They are so going down. We are taking them down."

I laughed and replied, "Damn, girl, who are you? You sound like me!"

On the par-3 sixth hole I hit one of my most important shots of the week, a 6-iron to four feet. That birdie cut the Euros' lead in half and got the crowd revved up, and after that it was the Michelle show. Something supernatural came over that girl and she played perfect golf the rest of the way, birdying the sixth, eighth, and ninth holes as we built our lead to 2 up. The better she played, the more demonstrative Michelle became, and combined with my usual theatrics—fist pumping, dancing, yelling at my ball and hers, et cetera—the crowd was in a tizzy. On the tenth hole Michelle was 182 yards out, in the rough, her ball below her feet, the pin tucked on the front of the green behind a bunker. She absolutely nuked a 6-iron to six feet. Even before the ball landed I said to my caddie Donny, "That is one of the most incredible shots I've ever seen in my life." Michelle's birdie put us 3 up.

No one enjoyed Michelle's stellar play more than her mom Bo and father B. J., who were living and dying with every shot. They followed us inside the ropes, as did my parents. It was funny to see them all chatting away in Korean. Michelle and I were both incredibly proud to wear the red, white, and blue, and having a pairing of KAPs—Captain Daniel loved to call us her Korean-American princesses—was a nice little reminder of the American melting pot.

We closed out the Euros on the fourteenth hole, a resounding 5 & 4 victory. Standing on the green, Michelle and I did a series of complicated high fives and handshakes and then we spontaneously started dancing. It wasn't choreographed, it was just raw and in the moment. At one point we were sort of grinding on each other and then Michelle smacked my ass. In front of thousands of people.

As soon as this lusty celebration was over, we were encircled by reporters. "I think this is the most fun I've ever had playing golf," Michelle said. "I'm still shaking from the round, it was just so much fun." I was so hoarse from all the hooting and hollering, it was a struggle to conduct the interviews.

There were still three taut matches going on behind us, so we jumped onto chauffeured golf carts and zigzagged around, cheering for our teammates. At some point word came down that I was going out in the afternoon for an alternate-shot match alongside Natalie. I considered heading back to the team room for a little rest, but it was so much fun cheering for the other girls I didn't want to miss a second of the action.

When all the morning matches concluded—knotting the Solheim Cup at six points apiece—I finally headed back toward the first tee for my match. During the cart ride I could feel for the first time how spent I was emotionally and physically. For a split second I considered telling Beth to play someone else for the good of the team. But she was showing so much confidence in me I didn't want to let her down, and I figured the adrenaline and amazing chemistry with Natalie would pull me along.

Unfortunately, we came out a little flat for the match while Becky Brewerton and Gwladys Nocera had fire in their eyes, birdying the first two holes to go 2 up. Natalie and I kept trying to generate some momentum, but neither of us could summon the right shot at the right time. It didn't help that our opponents were absolutely relentless, birdying the fifth hole to go 3 up and then birdying number six to push the lead to 4 up. We never mounted a rally and wound up getting spanked 5 & 4. Playing the final few holes knowing we were going to lose was gut-wrenching, and when the match was over I wept openly on the fourteenth green. The next day one of the local newspapers had a picture of me crying on the shoulder of assistant captain Kelly Robbins.

I was still pretty down that night at dinner, but my teammates were so positive and encouraging my mood eventually brightened. Anyway, there was no time to pout because the next day's action was going to be intense—the Solheim Cup was tied 8–8 after two days, meaning each of the twelve singles matches would be monumental.

Once again we had a raucous time announcing the pairings. Paula Creamer was going to be sent out first, which was no surprise—she's our little fire starter, always playing with so much heart and energy. I thought Beth would put me out in one of the first matches because numerous times during the week she had noted my ability to get the crowd fired up. I was so honored, then, that she saved me for the ninth match, a spot where the whole Solheim Cup could conceivably be decided. It made me feel like I was more than just a cheerleader. A tough opponent awaited in Tania Elosegui, who had played very well over the first two days. Was I a tad pumped up? When Beth announced the match I brought down the house by yelling, "Rookie going *doooowwwwnnnn!*"

The tension is unbearable for the Sunday singles at the Solheim. The matches tee off every ten minutes and the electricity just builds and builds, as roars cascade across the course and the endless momentum shifts are quantified in the scoreboards' red (for the U.S.) and blue. I wandered over to the first tee to watch the early matches play away, and it was such a memorable scene, with lots of flags being waved and chanting and cheering.

Tania and I halved the first hole with pars. On the par-5 second we both went for the green; she wound up in a greenside bunker, and I was in pretty good shape just off the edge of the putting surface. After Tania missed her fifteen-foot birdie putt, I had a six-footer for the win. Drawing first blood is huge psychologically. As important as the putt was, I felt completely peaceful standing over it, like there was no way I could miss. When my ball disappeared into the cup I threw one finger up in the air to signify I was 1 up. The crowd went bananas.

I bogeyed the fourth hole, squaring the match. Beth was waiting for me on the fifth tee. One of the things that made her such a standout captain was her preparation. She left nothing to chance. The par-3 fifth hole was 132 yards on the scorecard but Beth, having quizzed some girls in the earlier matches, informed me it was playing more like 140 due to the wind. I put away my 9-iron and went with the 8, sticking my tee shot to five feet. The gallery serenaded me with a chant of "Bir-die, bir-die, bir-die!" After I made the putt to win the hole I put my thumbs in my underarms and flapped like a bird.

I hit another great iron shot on six to go 2 up but Tania wasn't about to fold. On the par-5 seventh she decided to go for a green protected by water off a downhill, sidehill lie. She ripped a 3-wood to twenty feet. Yes, I was trying to beat her brains in, but I could still appreciate such a superb golf shot. I walked up to Tania and said, "Dude, that was awesome!" She looked at me funny, like she didn't know how to take it, but I was entirely sincere.

My eight-footer for birdie became moot when Tania buried her eagle putt. She left the ball in the hole for her caddie to collect, and as she strolled away she threw one finger up in the air, just as I had on number one. I later heard the announcers made a big deal of it on the telecast, but I didn't even see Tania do it as I was walking off the green and my back was turned. But it's all good—if you dish it out you gotta take it, too, and I have no trouble with someone strutting after making an eagle to win a hole in the Solheim Cup.

On eight I hit a bad tee shot, leading to a bogey that left us all square; the match was getting wilder and wilder, as only one of the seven previous holes had been halved. At this point in the day the scoreboard was bleeding blue, with Europe leading in seven of the twelve matches. With every passing hole my match was feeling more and more like life and death.

On number nine Tania was bunkered off the tee. Playing first from the fairway I hit a 9-iron to two feet. The cheering up by the green was thunderous, but Tania quieted the fans with an incredible 7-iron from the bunker that settled even closer to the hole than my ball. I gave her a high five and said, "Mad props, that was a beautiful shot." The birdies sent our match to the back nine still all square.

We halved ten, and I played the par-5 eleventh perfectly—leaving a twelve-foot birdie putt—which Tania conceded after she made a mess of the hole. I was back to 1 up. As we halved the next two holes I could hear a series of cheers rippling across Rich Harvest Farms as my teammates were staging inspired rallies. In the third match Michelle Wie was all square with Helen Alfredsson through fourteen holes but she won the fifteenth and sixteenth, ultimately taking the match 1 up to close a rousing debut during which she went 3–0–1. In match four Brittany Lang was 2 down with two holes to play to European warrior Laura Davies, the only player ever to compete in all eleven Solheims. But Brittany won the final two holes to steal a huge half point. In match five our emotional leader Juli Inkster was 2 down through thirteen holes to long-hitting Gwladys Nocera but went on a birdie binge to halve the match. Still, the Euros kept battling, getting lopsided victories in the sixth and eighth matches, adding to the sphincter factor of my tussle with Tania.

At the par-3 thirteenth hole my tee shot drifted a little right, catching a tree limb near the green. Tania hit a nice shot pin-high and I was thinking, *Dang, there goes my lead*. But I summoned a crazy-ass flop shot to four feet. Tania tapped in for par, leaving me a do-or-die putt. As I was standing over it, Fabolous popped into my head. It sounds silly, but hearing that music in my mind gave me a little shot of confidence. I made the putt and uncorked a big fist pump.

Number fourteen was a momentous hole. I was over the green with my approach shot, and a so-so chip left me eight feet to save par. Tania had a birdie putt to win the hole but she gunned it five feet past. So if I could make my putt, it would put a ton of pressure on her. I drained it, my fourth straight one-putt. I jumped in the air and did a little dance and the crowd started chanting, "U-S-A! K-I-M! U-S-A! K-I-M!" This outburst of emotion was spontaneous and instinctive, but I wish it hadn't happened because Tania still had to putt. It's okay to celebrate when you win a hole, but you never want to do anything to potentially disrupt your opponent. As soon as I came to my senses I raised my hands and asked the crowd to quiet down.

I don't know if Tania was affected or not but she missed her putt, losing the hole to send me 2 up. She betrayed no emotion but her caddie gave me the stink eye walking off the green.

I was still feeling a little bad about the whole thing on the sixteenth tee and I didn't do a good job of getting refocused. I hit a series of mediocre shots and Tania won the hole with a par to cut my lead in half. The sixteenth hole is a nasty par-3, demanding a carry over wetlands to an elevated, steeply sloped green. The pin was in a precarious spot in the back left corner. Tania hit first, a cautious shot to the front of the green that left her a very long birdie putt. I was between clubs—I wasn't sure a 6-iron would get there, but feared a 5-iron was too much stick. All week I had done a good job of playing by feel and not getting wrapped up in mechanical thoughts. Now I pictured in my mind a high, soft cut shot, starting at the left edge of the green and drifting back toward the flag. Without any second-guessing I opened the face of my 5-iron and let it rip. The strike was pure but as my ball was in the air I said, "Please God or Allah or Buddha, let this be the right club!" It was. My ball almost hit the flagstick and settled ten feet away. It was without a doubt one of the best, coolest shots of my life. Tania's ensuing birdie putt was very bold, running twelve feet by. Still away, she somehow stepped up and buried the putt, which was some of the most impressive shit I've seen in a long time. Then, after a few deep breaths, I hit an absolutely perfect putt, and when my ball tumbled into the hole the grandstand exploded and I yelled, "The Cup stays here!" I was now 2 up with two holes to play, meaning even if I lost the last two holes I would still bring home a half point. (Not that I was planning to let up.) Before leaving the green, I studied the leaderboard. Brittany Lincicome had recently closed out Sophie Gustafson 3 & 2. Her victory plus my guaranteed half point gave the U.S. 13½ points with four matches still on the course. So we needed only another half point. In match ten Cristie Kerr was all square with Maria Hjorth, and behind her Morgan Pressel was 1 up through fourteen versus Anna Nordqvist. It was no longer a question of whether we were going to win but rather who would have the glory of recording the clinching putt.

After two good drives on seventeen I hit first and played a so-so shot twenty-five feet short of the flag. Tania followed with a tremendous approach to four feet. I was just so impressed with this girl. I gave her another high five and said, "Dude, that shot was incredible. How much are you loving this right now?"

"Yeah, this is pretty special."

When I got up to the green I could see it was ringed by my teammates and hordes of reporters and various hangers-on. The crowd confirmed what I had already suspected: If I made my birdie putt, the Cup was ours. After all I'd been through this year, after the Tragedy of 2007, I couldn't stop thinking about how sweet it would be to make the putt and be mobbed by my teammates. I was practically playing the *SportsCenter* highlight in my mind. With all these distractions, I forgot to hit my putt hard enough and it expired two feet short. So lame. Tania made her birdie so we marched to the eighteenth hole, ceding the stage to Morgan Pressel. After birdying the fifteenth hole she made a 2 on sixteen, closing out Nordqvist and clinching the Cup for the United States. I got the word in the eighteenth fairway and was thrilled for Morgan and all of my teammates, but I was also determined to finish off my match in style. After a wayward drive I laid up and then hit a good shot onto the green to set up a birdie try. Tania's drive had gone way right, too. Trying a heroic recovery, she clipped a tree limb with her next shot and the ball bounced into the hazard. Eventually she conceded my birdie and I won the match by the score of 2 up, ending the week with a sparkly 3–1 record.

The last couple of matches finished up, and then it was pandemonium around the eighteenth green. We were all hugging and dancing and waving American flags at the crowd. At one point Michelle said to me, "I have tears in my eyes and I don't even know why."

"Welcome to the Solheim Cup, baby!" I screamed.

After an emotional closing ceremony, the team piled into a bus for a victory party in the ballroom at a Holiday Inn about ten miles away. Dan had taken off that morning, but my good friend Jan Meierling had flown in and we had a great time. The only people missing were the European players. Win or lose, those girls never skip a party, and we were all disappointed that they never showed up.

By midnight I was exhausted and so were all of my teammates, so we caught a bus back to Rich Harvest Farms. Arriving back at the cabins we could hear music and laughing and realized the Europeans had decided to stay on-site for their party. Even though I was completely knackered, I shouted, "I'm going to the Euro party—who's with me?"

No one, as it turned out, but I didn't care. When I rolled in, all the European players were so cool and welcoming and a couple of them said, "We knew you were the only one who would show up." It was now about one A.M. and the party had gotten very sloppy. One of the team's helpers had passed out drunk and was sprawled on the floor. The players had covered him with a tarp, encircled him with pylons, and taken police-style photos of the whole scene.

The party featured some bumping hip-hop music, and sometime around two thirty A.M. I spotted Tania Elosegui on the dance floor and went out and joined her. Twelve hours earlier, we had been locked in a battle for the ages. Now we were dancing and laughing together, bonded forever by the incredible experience of competing in the Solheim Cup.

CHAPTER 10

Aftermath

Following the European squad's party at the Solheim Cup, I returned to the cabin to pack up my stuff. When I was done it was four eighteen A.M. I lay down for exactly forty-two minutes and then the alarm went off. Portland was beckoning, for the Safeway Classic. A handful of my Solheim teammates were on the same flight; it was cool to be hanging out at the Chicago airport together, having so many fans come up to express their excitement about our victory. That was just a prelude to all the backslapping that awaited in Portland. Everywhere I went my first few days at the tournament, all anybody wanted to talk about was the Solheim Cup. Yani Tseng is very proud to be from Taiwan, but when I saw her she said, "Man, that looked like so much fun—I wish I was American!"

Unfortunately, not all of the feedback was so positive. There were about a half dozen people on Twitter who were bashing my comportment during the Solheim Cup, basically calling me a poor sport. I fired back with some spicy replies, and all the

back-and-forth wound up getting regurgitated at golfdigest
.com. The reader comments section at that site and others were
ablaze with opinions about me, and some of them were less
than polite. I was also annoyed by some of the things in the
print media. Dottie Pepper, the former player turned TV an-
nouncer, said in her weekly column in *Sports Illustrated* that I
had "Ochocinco syndrome," referring to the flamboyant NFL
receiver Chad Ochocinco (né Johnson). Pepper added, "I know
Christina Kim loves the galleries and is a ham, but she should
be a little more respectful of the game. In the NFL she'd have
been given eighteen excessive celebration penalties."

What bothered me about this kind of criticism is that I acted
exactly the same way in 2005, and back then everyone celebrated my "enthusiasm" and "passion." I'm always emotional
on the golf course and everyone knows it, so why was my fist
pumping and cheerleading such a big deal all of the sudden?
What was especially weird to me was that these vocal fans and
reporters were more bent out of shape than my opponents. At
the conclusion of the Solheim Cup the entire European team
was brought into the media center and a muckraking British
scribe asked a very leading question: "For anyone who would
care to answer, did Christina Kim get under your skin a little at
any point this week?" The reporter was obviously trying to stir
up a controversy that could have been helpful to the European
players, as it might deflect some of the blame for the loss. (European captain Mark James employed this tactic at the 1999
Ryder Cup when he made a big deal of criticizing the American
players' spontaneous celebrations after Justin Leonard holed
his famous putt.) But at the Solheim press conference none of
the players took the bait. The woman who spoke up was Laura

Davies, one of the bluntest chicks on the planet. If she had been upset she would have said so, but Davies replied, "She's a lovely girl. She's excitable. That's the way it is. She's good fun. She gets the crowds going. Good luck to her." Those words meant a lot to me, but all the criticism still stung. I'm a professional athlete, yes, but I'm also a sensitive woman. Being on the LPGA Tour is not like playing for the Yankees, where getting ripped is a daily part of the job. We don't get a ton of coverage, and so, with the exception of Michelle Wie, none of us have a lot of practice at being a media punching bag. My first few days in Portland I was definitely a little bummed out that anyone would think I disrespected the European players, whom I hold in such high regard and who were so welcoming to me at their party.

My mood probably wasn't helped by my caddie situation. Once again I was looking for a new looper. Donny had informed me during the run-up to the Solheim Cup that he had been offered a chance to caddie for Danny Lee, and of course he said yes. Lee is a can't-miss kid who could easily be the number-two player in the world in a few years. At the 2008 U.S. Amateur, when Lee was eighteen, he broke Tiger Woods's record en route to becoming the event's youngest champion, and then in February 2009, while still competing as an amateur, Lee beat all the pros at the prestigious Johnnie Walker Classic, making him the youngest champion in the history of the European Tour. Lee wanted Donny to begin working for him the week of the Solheim Cup, but, to Donny's credit, he said he couldn't leave me in the lurch. Saying good-bye to Donny at the closing ceremony was pretty sad for me—he's a great caddie and such a cool guy, and I learned a lot from him in our short time together.

So on Tuesday in Portland I had the dispiriting chore of trying to find a fill-in for the week. The pro at the host venue,
Pumpkin Ridge Golf Club, hooked me up with Jim Dunlap, the
reigning club champion who had his amateur status reinstated
after having played a few years on the pro minitours. Jim knew
golf and had a mellow vibe I liked. And at six foot four, 220
pounds, he definitely had a presence about him. That afternoon
we played nine holes with Brittany Lincicome, who is one of
the tour's biggest practice-round sharks. I don't do a lot of bet-
ting early in the week—there's enough pressure once the tournament begins—but Brittany loves to gamble, and she talked
me into playing five-dollar birdies. Over the first eight holes she
was skunked and I was up fifteen dollars. On the tee of the
ninth hole, a reachable par-5, she proposed we play twenty-
dollar eagles. I reluctantly agreed. So of course Brittany made
an eagle and I wound up owing her five bones. Jim loved the
camaraderie. In our efforts to get to know each other better, it
helped that he and I had an extra practice round together, since
the Safeway is one of a handful of fifty-four-hole tournaments
we play during the year. (The decision to play three rounds as
opposed to four is usually dictated by the sponsor—specifically,
whether or not it wants an extra day of pro-ams for entertaining
clients.) I don't have a strong preference for either format, but
in the fifty-four-hole events I tend to play more aggressively because there is not that extra round to make up ground if you
post a mediocre score.

For the first round of the Safeway I was paired with Catriona Matthew, the supermom who had outdueled me at the
Women's British Open and is one of the stalwarts of the European Solheim Cup team. It was a good pairing because I was

still in the Solheim mind-set. On the first hole of the first round—the par-5 tenth, as we teed off on the back nine—Catriona made a longish birdie putt and I had a five-footer for a bird of my own. All I could think was, *I can't let her win the hole*. I made the putt.

Through eleven holes I was even par, just kind of moseying along, not feeling overly spunky due to a nasty head cold. (A lot of the girls got sick after the Solheim, which is such a grueling physical test.) Then I birdied number three and at the fourth hole rolled in an improbable forty-footer with about eight feet of break. I bogeyed five but came back on six with another terrific iron shot. Ho-hum, another birdie. I was still on such a high from the Solheim Cup that the game just seemed easy all of sudden. Eight and nine are both par-5s and I got up and down at each, closing with three straight birdies and five in my final seven holes. My four-under-par 68 left me in eleventh place.

During the second round I made five more birdies en route to a 70 that moved me up to a tie for ninth. I was four strokes off the lead but felt very much in contention to win, especially because Pumpkin Ridge's Ghost Creek course has five par-5s and I could reach all of them. The Solheim Cup had given me my first taste of victory in a long time and I was hungry to win another tournament. That night, while lying in bed, I practiced a victory speech in my mind.

I was pumped up from the very first hole on Sunday, rolling in a fifteen-footer for birdie followed by a couple of big fist pumps. Take that, haters. On the par-3 third hole I hit a nice tee shot to twelve feet. While I was waiting for my turn to putt, my playing partner Sophie Gustafson knocked in a forty-footer for birdie and then M. J. Hur made a thirty-foot putt for par. Jeez, tough crowd. Duly inspired, I made my birdie and we all exchanged high fives. At both the par-5 eighth and ninth holes I went for the green and just missed, but each time I got up and down for birdie, pushing my score to −10. I was playing great but barely keeping up: Michele Redman had birdied four of the first eight holes to get to −12, while Suzann Pettersen birdied three of the first five to reach −11.

On the tenth hole I hit a sweet drive and then a perfect 3-wood to within twenty feet of the hole for a very doable eagle try. The tenth green is adjacent to the first green, where Morgan Pressel happened to be at that moment. After I buried my putt Morgan started clapping and pumping her fist, yelling, "Yeah, partner!" That was so cool.

I had played my first ten holes in six under par. At −12 I was tied for the lead, but I didn't know it because of the dearth of on-course scoreboards. Still, there was no doubt I was in the thick of things. Unfortunately, there was a big traffic jam on the tee of the par-3 eleventh, and standing around for fifteen minutes was the worst thing that could have happened to me. I lost all that great momentum from the eagle, and during the tedious wait thoughts of winning kept creeping into my head, even though I was trying as hard as I could to only focus on the shot at hand. If you want to guarantee you won't win a golf tournament, all you have to do is think about winning it. The only way to survive the Sunday pressure is to get lost in the process of hitting good shots and not worry about the result. My old caddie Donny was great at reading my mood and keeping me focused.

Jim Dunlap had done a terrific job for a newbie, but we were still just getting to know each other and, standing there on the eleventh tee, my nervousness intensifying by the minute, there wasn't much he could say. When at long last it was time to hit, I made a hurried swing and pulled my tee shot left of the green. An okay chip left me seven feet to save par. For the first time all week I felt a little jittery over a putt. I backed off to get refocused, and then did it a second time. I still missed. Bogey. My playing partner M. J. Hur, a shy, unassuming nineteen-year-old Korean, was in the midst of a torrid stretch—she had gone birdie, birdie, eagle on the par-5s, and when she birdied eleven she had tied me at 11 under par. Then she birdied twelve, too. Behind us Suzann Pettersen, one of the game's most explosive players, was on a streak of her own, birdying nine and ten to get to −13.

All week long I had enjoyed an enviable mental clarity, just focusing on one shot at a time. All of a sudden I was trying to keep up with M. J. and stressing about the leaderboard. Just as it had at the British Open, this tension affected my putting stroke. I was still hitting quality shots but the putts stopped going in, and it only got worse after M. J. birdied fourteen to get to −13. On the fifteenth hole I missed a five-footer for birdie and at sixteen I blew a birdie putt that was even shorter, leaving me stuck at −11. According to the scoreboard I had seen on the sixteenth hole, Suzann was at −14. I had no idea she was on her way to double-bogeying number fifteen.

For the final round, the tees on the seventeenth hole had been pushed way up, shortening the par-4 to a mere 220 yards to entice players into going for a green guarded by water and bunkers. My first instinct was to lay up. I had lost some confidence during the back nine and it was an awkward shot because I was between clubs, afraid my rescue wouldn't carry the water but wary of going long with my 3-wood. There was another long wait on the seventeenth tee and I got increasingly antsy—and greedy. The more I thought about it, the more I wanted that eagle opportunity, so I decided to try to reach the green by taking a little off my 3-wood. Had Donny been there, maybe he would have talked me out of it, but we'll never know. I hit the 3-wood long and left, into a terrible lie on a steep slope. My pitch came out very hot and ran through the green to within a couple inches of the lake, leaving a very dicey chip. I left it ten feet short and then missed the putt, taking bogey.

I was so done mentally at that point it's no surprise I bogeyed eighteen, too. My 69 left me in a tie for eighth, ultimately four strokes back of a three-way play-off between M. J., Suzann, and Michele Redman, which M. J. won on the second extra hole for her first LPGA victory. A birdie-birdie finish would have, theoretically, gotten me into the play-off. One of the lessons I took from the loss is that I need to trust my first instinct. Laying up at seventeen would have been the correct play, and if I had been disciplined enough to do it, who knows how the last two holes might have played out.

My top finishes at the Kraft Nabisco and Women's British felt like moral victories, but this near miss stung quite a bit more. I earned $38,830 to move to thirty-eighth on the money list, but even that cute little check came with regrets—a simple par-par finish would have brought me another $40K. My two victories came so early in my career, I don't think I properly appreciated how hard it is to win out here. With my title drought at four years and counting, I was now brutally, painfully aware of it.

The morning after the conclusion of the Safeway I was up at the ungodly hour of three thirty A.M. to catch a ride to the airport. My destination was Calgary for the Canadian Women's Open. Playing for a national championship is a big deal, and the folks in Canada run a five-star event. The Open moves around the country from year to year, so this was my first visit to Calgary. I had no idea it was Canada's version of the Wild West. Everyone drives pickup trucks and wears cowboy hats, and the city is framed by lovely rolling hills dotted with bales of hay.

Two days before the tournament began, I was part of a racy photo shoot for *ESPN The Magazine*'s Body Issue, which was to feature PG-13 pictures of nude athletes from a variety of sports. When I was initially contacted about participating, just before the Solheim Cup, I was a bit wary, but eventually I couldn't help but feel flattered, like this was a nice public acknowledgment that I was no longer medically obese. Still, it was a little intimidating when I found out the pictures would include fellow LPGA players Sandra Gal, who is very tall and glamorous, and Minea Blomqvist, owner of one of the best asses on tour. A couple days before the shoot Minea had to pull out, but her replacement, Anna Grzebien, was no less of a babe, a size 2 with long legs and ripped abs.

The shoot took place at a local golf course that was being renovated and was thus deserted. Unfortunately, no one seemed to realize until too late that the chosen setting was flanked by a fairly busy road and the course's trees and shrubs did not entirely block the view of the three of us. So Sandra, Anna, and I had to step into our robes every time a car or jogger or biker passed by. When the coast was clear, we'd drop trou and get back in place for a flurry of photos. It was, as you might imagine, a bit nerve-racking. So, too, was the fact that we were not granted control of the images. In the shots my breasts and hoo-ha are smooshed against a golf bag and thus out of sight, but the three of us wouldn't know how the finished pictures looked until the magazine hit newsstands a month later.

The other big development of the early part of the week was now becoming a little too familiar: breaking in a new caddie. My sixth looper of the year was Mike Bestor, whom I had been put in touch with by my old caddie Donny. Mike had packed on the LPGA ages ago, but in recent years was concentrating on the PGA Tour. Mike was available for a few weeks because his guy, Dean Wilson, did not qualify for the PGA Tour's FedEx Cup play-off events. Mike and I spent the practice rounds trying to figure out yardages. Priddis Greens Golf & Country Club is at an elevation of about forty-two hundred feet; in the thin air the ball travels farther, although the carry is not always consistent. A high shot with a lot of backspin, like a cut 9-iron, might go an extra 6 percent, but a low, hard draw with a 4-iron might carry only an extra 3 percent. With Mike just beginning to learn my game there was a lot of guesswork with the yardages, which was stressing me out.

The uncertainty over club selection was hardly the only reason why my first-round 75 was such a disaster. The day before, I had started my period, which is an unpleasant fact of life for a female professional athlete. Anyone who has sisters or daughters knows that in close proximity women's cycles will become linked, and that definitely happens on tour. If you go to the range during that time of the month and say, "Ew, I feel icky today," a half dozen girls will pipe up, "I know, right?" Swinging at a hundred miles an hour doesn't feel so good when you're cramping, and I know a few players who lose clubhead speed when they're on their period. I don't have any physical issues like that, but being on the rag definitely affects me emotionally. My decision making on the course is sometimes a bit rash, and in general I have less patience. Slow play is always irritating, but during that time of the month it drives me absolutely batty.

So I was already in a little bit of a delicate state prior to my first round in Calgary, but my dad made it a helluva lot worse on the drive to the course. We hadn't yet talked about the disappointing finish in Portland a few days earlier and, unsolicited, he began offering his critique. He was trying to be tactful, and any other time I probably wouldn't have been so defensive, but everything he said felt like he was attacking me and we bickered throughout the entire thirty-minute drive. By the time we got to the course, I was raging. As I stood on the tee box of the first hole, Dad called me over and wrapped me in a hug, but it was too little too late. As we played the first hole I told my caddie Mike, "I'm on my period, my dad and I just had a huge fight, so I want to apologize in advance for being an überbitch." I'm quite sure the poor guy has never gotten that speech from Dean Wilson. My bad attitude certainly didn't help me on the golf course: I made four bogeys and a double, along the way cursing and slamming clubs and generally acting like a crabby brat. My dad was waiting behind the eighteenth hole, and the first thing I hissed when I saw him was "I told you I was gonna play like shit! See what you get for upsetting me!"

For the second round I decided to just get over myself. I had a much better attitude and more cheerful disposition. I was also more confident with the yardage numbers, and the result was a stellar 66, a score bettered by only four players on the day. I surged from 112th place to 30th.

Feeling perkier, I partook in that night's tournament party at a country-western bar. All the players were decked out in jeans and cowboy hats—I had lugged my own from Orlando—and a dozen of us took spins on a mechanical bull. It was good fun, despite the slightly strained bicep and the chafing I suffered on my inner thighs.

During the third round I made five birdies but somehow still shot a one-over-par 72, a score I matched on Sunday thanks to double bogeys on the fourth and eighteenth holes, which ultimately left me in thirty-third place. It was a sloppy week, and fatigue was definitely a factor. There were times when I felt exhausted on the golf course, the cumulative effect of my wild nights in New York City followed by the grind of the Solheim Cup and then a series of very early tee times in Portland necessitated by TV time slots. I was also frazzled from having my parents travel with me for a third straight week, which hadn't happened in years. From Calgary I was journeying to Rogers, Arkansas, for the P&G Beauty NW Arkansas Championship. I would be on my own for a change and was really looking forward to a mellow week.

Driving out from the Rogers airport you can see (and smell) an endless number of chicken coops and it's like, Yep, we're in Arkansas. But across from the player hotel is one of the nicest malls I've ever visited, full of super high-end boutiques. This part of Arkansas is home to the tournament title sponsor Procter & Gamble as well as Wal-Mart and Tyson Chicken. There's a lot of money and plenty of sophisticated golf aficionados, but at the same time many of the locals and tourney volunteers are down-home and country, which gives the tournament its color and sense of place.

My first few days in Arkansas did not bring the mellowness I was hoping for. Word had leaked out about the ESPN photo shoot, and once again I was getting slammed in the media. Ron Sirak, the dean of LGPA scribes, wrote in *GolfWorld*, "The issue of how to market sexuality has always been a hot-button issue for the LPGA. Many players fear that doing anything that takes the focus off them as professional athletes will provide ammunition to those who like to poke fun at the tour. Several players, speaking anonymously, were troubled by the fact that Kim is a player representative on the LPGA Board of Directors, feeling her involvement sent the wrong message and implied member support of the photos." Steve Elling of cbssportsline .com wrote, "I defended Kim and her over-the-top antics at the Solheim Cup because the game needs more color. But removing her top is another matter altogether. The LPGA can't have it both ways. On one hand, they say issues like sexual preference shouldn't matter in this enlightened age. Then three players turn around and use their sexuality as a salacious marketing tool? I'm no prude, but I just don't get it. Kim is a big, bawdy girl with a self-deprecating wit who cracks boob jokes and can swear like a longshoreman, but I can't see how this will enhance her popularity. At least, not in any way that helps."

In fact, LPGA officials had given their blessing to the photo shoot, which was pointed out in the *GolfWorld* story. "We were briefed on the concept by the [ESPN] editors, and felt comfortable with it given the fun idea as well as the fact that numerous other leagues and sports also participated," LPGA chief communications officer David Higdon told Sirak. "We support and encourage all our appealing, personable athletes to promote themselves and their sport in the process. No group of pro athletes in all of sport offer fans a more diverse range of interesting personalities, and we want to showcase this huge asset to not just golf fans but sports fans worldwide. Working with *ESPN The Magazine* and their world-class editors and photographers was a tremendous opportunity that we're glad our players carefully considered and then chose to pursue."

Once again I was left scratching my head about the contradictions inherent in the criticism. LPGA players are often derided as emotionless robots, but when I get fired up at the Solheim Cup it's somehow a bad thing. Now dozens of athletes from numerous sports are participating in a highly anticipated special issue for a respected publication but I'm getting singled out as some kind of bad example. And the backdrop to all of this is the LPGA's struggles to garner mainstream attention. It seems like no matter what you do, you can't win.

I wish the distraction created by all the unpleasantness in the press could be blamed for my erratic performance in Arkansas, but that wouldn't be quite accurate. I played well in spurts but just made way too many mistakes. During the first round I eagled the fourteenth hole, my seventh big bird of the year, a total which to that point in the season had been bettered by only seven players. Still, my one-over-par 72 left me in seventy-third place. I followed with a very clean second round, making only one bogey during a 68 that propelled me all the way to twenty-fourth, but my final round was a mess. I closed the front nine by going bogey, birdie, bogey, triple bogey, the latter coming when my approach shot trickled into a bunker and it took me three humiliating tries to excavate myself from the sand. Three bogeys in a row on the back nine doomed me to fifty-fourth place.

It's funny how the Solheim Cup affects players differently. Suzann Pettersen went only 1–4 for Europe, but the loss seemed to galvanize her: She followed her play-off defeat in Canada by roaring to victory in Arkansas, putting herself in the mix for the LPGA Player of the Year award. I got a similar boost in Portland but never really recovered from kicking away that tournament. Throw in two unpleasant media controversies plus my monthly visitor, and I left Arkansas flat worn out, emotionally and physically.

CHAPTER 11

Homecoming Queen

On September 14 I left Arkansas and returned to Orlando after having been gone for a full month. Stepping inside my house induced a weird letdown. It felt like returning to a six-bedroom storage facility, not a real home. I had moved to Florida because of the geographical convenience to many tournaments, the lack of state income tax, and, after having spent my whole life in California, the desire for a change of scenery. But after five years away, I was missing Cali. No doubt these feelings were intensified because the LPGA was in the midst of a two-week swing through the Golden State. Immediately after Arkansas was the Samsung World Championship, the super-exclusive event with only twenty top players in the field, played at Torrey Pines in San Diego. The week after that would bring the CVS/pharmacy LPGA Challenge, in the Bay Area, always one of the most important weeks of the year for me because it's my hometown event.

I wasn't allowed past the velvet rope at Torrey Pines, which was fine. The preceding month had been so wearying, I needed some time to veg. But after three days of relaxing in Orlando, I couldn't shake that feeling of not belonging. I'm a wanderer at heart, and maybe nowhere but a Marriott will ever feel like home. Orlando sure as hell didn't, so on something of a whim I flew to New York City.

I did a lot of shopping and strolling during one glorious afternoon in the city, but there was also business to discuss. My agents are based in Connecticut, and we got together to finalize the details of my endorsement deal with PUR water filters. It's a healthy amount of money, but more important to me is the chance to spread the word about PUR's products and in some small way help the planet's dire water problems. My agents also briefed me on some advanced discussions with a business-services company. It was kind of cool that corporations were suddenly eager to align themselves with me, warts and all.

During my time in New York I also sat down with a couple of editors at *ESPN The Magazine*, a meeting I had initiated. My relationship with the media had become increasingly contentious going back to the twenty-five-hundred-dollar fine for dropping the f-bomb in Hawaii at the start of the year. I had resolved to try to establish better lines of communication and ESPN seemed like a logical place to start, given my uneasiness with the recent nude photo shoot. The Body Issue had not yet hit newsstands but the editors gave me a sneak peek of the pictures of myself, Sandra Gal, and Anna Grzebien, and I have to say they were pretty damn hot. We had some very constructive conversations, and the ESPN guys said they hoped to get me back in the magazine soon—with clothes—so it was definitely a fruitful meeting.

After a day and a half in New York I flew into Oakland to begin my preparations for the CVS. For my first night in town, that meant playing poker and drinking Tanqueray and tonics with a half dozen of my boys. I've known most of these guys since my early teens, either from school or the NorCal golf scene. They always watch me play when the LPGA is in town and we have so much fun hanging out in the evenings. Being around these old friends only made me more certain that I belonged back in California.

During the poker game I solved my caddie situation for the week by talking my buddy Will Hornby into taking the job. We've played a lot of golf together going back to when I was sixteen, so he knows my game and we have very good chemistry. The early part of the week wasn't ideal for preparing for the tournament, because on Tuesday I had to endure an LPGA board meeting from seven thirty A.M. to three P.M. There was only time for nine holes afterward, but it turned out to be a momentous practice round. Playing through the late-afternoon shadows on a familiar golf course—Blackhawk Country Club in Danville—gave me such a sense of serenity. It was the same peacefulness I felt at the British Open, which had been sparked by one swing of my 5-iron. At Blackhawk there was another defining moment. On the eleventh hole I hit a hybrid of such purity it imbued me with an enveloping sense of confidence. I get this feeling a few times every season, and there's never a good explanation for how or why it magically appears. It transcends golf. I can be so self-conscious and insecure—not as a player but as a human being—but once in a while I discover peace of mind and it seeps into my game. Being back in NorCal among friends and family definitely had that effect on me. After that glorious hybrid, I knew I was going to have a good week.

I birdied the third hole of my first round, setting off a huge roar in my gallery. My dad loves to big-time it when I'm playing in Danville, so he had seven or eight of his cronies with him. Throw in my half dozen guy friends, and my personal rooting section was obnoxiously loud, even as I cooled off, playing the first ten holes in a mere even par. On the par-5 eleventh I gave my gallery something to really yell about. An aggressive drive allowed me to cut the corner of the dogleg, and then from 203 yards out another good swing with my hybrid left me just off the back of the green. I played a delicate chip that tracked right into the hole for a thrilling eagle. That keyed my round of two-under-par 70, which left me in twentieth place, a pretty solid start.

Afterward I got a hug from my friend Erik. I've had a huge crush on him since I was twelve years old, when he was one of the best local golfers and I'd follow him around like a puppy dog. It was always unrequited, or so I thought, but on my first night in Cali he admitted to having had some feelings for me back in the day. Granted, it was four thirty A.M. when Erik made the admission and we'd both had a few too many adult beverages, but it was still an intriguing piece of information, and in the days afterward the vibe between us became a lot flirtier. This may or may not have been a contributing factor to a phone conversation I had with Meg Mallon's nephew Dan, ending our miniromance. I hadn't seen Dan since the Solheim Cup, and the logistics weren't working out. He's a great person and I know we're always going to be friends, but my heart wasn't in trying to pursue a long-distance relationship. I'm not chasing love right now. I'm working hard at loving myself. If a guy wants to hang out and we can love me together, great. I wasn't sure what to make of the whole Erik thing, but it was definitely exciting to have him in the gallery and yet another reason for me to want to play well.

Unfortunately, my second round didn't go exactly as planned. I started the day with a birdie on the tenth hole—my round began on the back nine—but then double-bogeyed the fourteenth when I dumped my approach shot into a hazard. It was a bad swing but also a mental error because I had lost my focus due to the painfully slow play of my partner, Sandra Gal. Slow play always upsets my rhythm. You have to wait and wait and wait and wait, and then when it's finally time to hit you're so antsy it's hard to slow down and go through your routine properly. A string of pars followed the double bogey and I finally generated some momentum with birdies on numbers three, five, and six, but then I made another ruinous double bogey on the seventh hole. This one I blame on the heavens. Just as I struck my shot, a huge gust of wind came up, knocking my ball down into a hazard short of the green. I looked up to the sky and said, "God, why did you do that to me?" No answer. My very uneven 73 dropped me to thirty-ninth place.

The alarm went off at five A.M. for the third round and I kept telling myself that a good score would allow me to sleep in the next day. Starting again on number ten—a long par-3—I struck a really pure 5-iron and, just like that, the magical feeling of peace and serenity returned. (It also helped that I had new playing partners in Hall of Famer Karrie Webb and Dee D'Alessio—they're cool chicks and, more to the point, they both play quite briskly.) I made a routine birdie on the par-5 eleventh hole and then on thirteen and fourteen hit beautiful iron shots to set up two more birds. I kept rolling with a fifteen-footer for another birdie on number one. I was having so much fun out there—my gallery was going crazy and my caddie Will kept me laughing, talking about funny old stories and our many shared friends. On the par-5 third hole I was just short of the green in two and hit a gorgeous flop shot that took one hop, flew into the hole, rattled around for a second, and then popped out, hanging on the lip. I wanted the eagle so much but settled for another birdie. On the par-5 fifth I smashed a 3-wood to twelve feet. My eagle putt looked good the whole way but somehow lipped out. Dang, I could have had two eagles in the span of about twenty minutes! You know you're playing some spectacular golf when birdies are disappointing. I birdied the short par-4 sixth, too, with a very sporty pitch. It added up to seven birdies against no bogeys for a smooth 65, my best round of the year. That shot me to a tie for ninth, and I got to sleep in for the final round.

The second I awoke on Sunday my nerves were jangling. It wasn't about being afraid of choking, as I didn't really have a realistic chance to win—at nine under par, I was seven strokes back of coleaders Lorena Ochoa and Sophie Gustafson. I knew there would be huge crowds because I was to be paired with local sweetheart Paula Creamer, but I was looking forward to that. The tension I was feeling had more to do with the third playing partner in our group, Maria Hjorth. Actually, it had nothing to do with Maria and everything to do with her caddie: my ex-boyfriend Mark. I hadn't seen him on a golf course since the final round of the Kraft Nabisco Championship five and a half months earlier. During our time together, Mark had become very friendly with all of my NorCal homies who would be in the gallery. I was freaked out that it would be awkward and weird to have everybody in such close proximity.

On the first tee Mark was very casual, and that helped relax me a tiny bit, but my swing still felt tight and tense. I hit a bad drive and went on to make bogey. Somehow I birdied the second hole, but I wasn't swinging nearly as aggressively as the day before. I eked out three pars and then made another bogey on six. I was so crestfallen, like, Am I really going to stink it up in front of all my friends and family?

Luckily, Will got me out of my funk by reminding me of our practice-round encounter with Paula Creamer. She has a global following, of course, but Paula is especially big in NorCal, as she hails from Pleasanton. We all grew up very aware of her legend. On Wednesday Will and I had bumped into Paula on the tee of a par-3 and I introduced them. As she was walking away Will was like, "I'm sorry, your name was?" Paula looked utterly dumbfounded, and I was so proud of Will for tweaking her like that.

On the eighth hole I hit a sweet approach shot to eight feet and finally got a putt to drop, a birdie that gave me a big shot of confidence. I played great from then on, making three more birdies without a bogey. One of the birds came on the par-4 seventeenth. It was playing 310 yards downhill so I decided to try to drive the green. Yeah, I was showing off a little bit. I summoned one of the best tee shots of my life, ripping it to within twenty feet of the flag. My 69 happened to be two shots better than Paula and left me tied for ninth, my third top-ten finish in my last five starts dating to the Women's British Open. Afterward my ex-boyfriend offered some very nice words of encouragement, and I was pleased that we're both mature enough to have a respectful working relationship.

The next day I began my journey to Prattville, Alabama, for the Navistar LPGA Classic. Waiting around San Jose International—my travel portal for years and years—it hit me that I felt more at home in that airport than in my house in Orlando.

The Navistar is played at the Senator course, which is part of the Robert Trent Jones Golf Trail that snakes across Alabama. It's a stunning venue and a fun week for the players because we all stay at the on-site hotel, which leads to a lot of kibitzing. On the eve of the tournament I went out to dinner with Michelle Wie and Jeehae Lee and we stuffed ourselves with shrimp and grits, mac 'n' cheese, fried okra, biscuits and gravy, and banana pudding. Good eatin'! The week before, Michelle had begun her third year at Stanford. (She carries a full load of classes in the fall and winter quarters but takes an annual leave of absence in the spring, allowing her to play a pretty complete LPGA schedule and still work toward her communications degree.) Michelle loves living in Palo Alto and was so excited to hear me talking about moving back to NorCal. Of course, housing prices are a lot more expensive there than in Orlando, but I was suddenly feeling a little less worried about money, and not just because my recent run of good play had taken me to thirty-sixth on the money list (with $325K). If the story of the summer was the unrelenting gloom and doom about the health of the LPGA—culminating in the departure of commissioner Carolyn Bivens—the early fall featured a steady stream of good news. During our week in Alabama, Navistar (a manufacturer of trucks and diesel engines) announced it was renewing its sponsorship deal for 2010. That came on the heels of similar commitments from the Wegmans LPGA, the Jamie Farr Classic, and the P&G NW Arkansas Championship. Rolex had also signed on to be a presenting sponsor to the 2009 Tour Championship. When the Bivens drama went down, the LPGA had only fifteen solid tournaments committed for 2010. Now tour officials were saying they expected to have as many as twenty-five events on the '10 schedule. This was a huge relief to all of the players, obviously. I always had faith in the LPGA leadership, but it was certainly comforting to know that I'd be gainfully employed in 2010 and beyond.

After the first round of the Navistar it looked as though I was headed for another big payday, as I shot a bogeyless 68 to put myself in sixteenth place. (I was four strokes off the lead but only two back of third place.) My score could have been a lot lower, too, if I had converted more of my numerous birdie chances. Putting is always a challenge on the Senator course—the greens are huge and undulating and the Bermuda grass is very grainy, so it's hard to read the putts and consistently get your speed correct. Growing up in Cali I never putted on Bermuda grass, and it often baffles me because the direction the grain is growing has a huge effect on the speed and break of putts. To serve as my caddie for the week I hired Steve Shellard, who used to work for the wonderfully named Shanshan Feng. Sensing my uncertainty, Steve tried to read a few putts for me early in the round, but I called him off. The reason all the caddie turnover hadn't bothered me too much is that I'm a pretty independent golfer: I like to calculate my own yardages and read my own putts. Even when I'm struggling to read them correctly.

My putter was cold throughout a second-round 73. On Saturday I had a pretty hot round going—four under par through twelve holes—but three-putts on the fifteenth and sixteenth doomed me to a ho-hum 70. For the final round I was even par through thirteen holes and then caught a series of bad breaks on the fourteenth, making a double bogey. That pissed me off so much I birdied the next three holes, finishing with a 71 that left me in twenty-seventh place, worth $10,735.

That evening I flew out of Alabama but, thankfully, I wasn't headed to boring old Orlando. The season may have been winding down, but some far-flung adventures were about to begin.

CHAPTER 12

An Innocent Abroad

Tournaments in Hawaii and China were to be played back-to-back in mid-October until a lack of corporate sponsorship led to their cancellation months earlier, leaving a hole in the LPGA schedule. Instead of sitting around for three weeks, I lined up a sweet working vacation: the Ladies Italian Open, on the outskirts of Milan. The Italian Open was being conducted by the Ladies European Tour (LET), which in 2009 would offer twenty-two tournaments with a total purse of just under ten million euros, or roughly fifteen million U.S. dollars. (By comparison, in '09 the LPGA had twenty-seven tournaments worth $47.6 million.) Every LET event sets aside one spot for the highest player in the world ranking who is otherwise not in the field. At the deadline to commit to the Italian Open, I was forty-fifth in the world; since none of the girls ahead of me wanted to play, I got in.

My flight to Milan was leaving out of New York City four days after the Navistar LPGA Classic ended in Alabama.

Rather than go home to Orlando I hung out in New York City instead, crashing at Cristie Kerr's fab three-bedroom apartment in the West Village. Until this summer I hadn't spent much time in New York, but after three glorious days of shopping and strolling and enjoying the nightlife I decided it's now my favorite city in the world. Sorry, Singapore.

While I was in New York I continued to exchange very flirty text messages with my old crush Erik. Part of me wished I was back in Northern California to see where this might lead, but the schedule wasn't going to allow it. This wasn't the first (or last) time golf would get in the way of romantic possibilities.

At least I had Italy to look forward to. It was such an exciting destination because I'd never been there, despite all of my world travels. My overnight flight arrived on Friday, October 9. By the time I reached my hotel room, my phone had practically melted. Turns out this was the day that *ESPN The Magazine* unveiled its Body Issue, and the comments began pouring in, from friends, fellow players, Twitter followers, and various randoms. The response was overwhelmingly positive, and even my dad—who understandably had not been that thrilled by the whole idea—grudgingly admitted the photo was tastefully done.

After a long nap at my hotel I journeyed to the Duomo in Milan at dusk. This was my first experience with classic Italian architecture, and it was so beautiful I had tears in my eyes. The next morning my madcap tour of Italy began, during which I crammed three weeks' worth of sightseeing into thirty-six hours. It started with an early-morning train ride to Florence. Outside the Uffizi I sat at a café and, wanting to feel Italian, ordered a

caprese salad and cappuccino. Who cared if it wasn't yet ten
A.M.? Inside the museum I was again overwhelmed by the
beauty of it all. I probably spent a full half hour staring at the
Botticelli painting *The Birth of Venus*, and again the tears flowed.
After my wondrous day in Florence, I caught a train to Rome.
Upon arriving I had a magical tour of some of the sights under
the lights, including the Colosseum and the Trevi Fountain.

Thanks to Twitter, it didn't feel like traveling alone. I posted
a running diary of my journey, with pictures, and the comments and suggestions kept pouring in. At the urging of a couple followers I hired a private guide for my time in Rome, and
he and I did all the must-dos. My favorite spot was the Roman
Forum—that Temple of Saturn was jaw-dropping, and I had
chills standing in the chamber of the old Senate. I fell in love
with the city and was sad to have to leave after just one long
day, but the golf tournament was beckoning. The last train back
to Milan ultimately got me to my hotel around midnight on
that Sunday. Having seen and done so much in so little time, I
was both exhausted and exhilarated. How dazzling was Italy? In
two days I had taken more than a thousand photographs.

It was fun checking in at the tournament on Monday afternoon. All the girls were like, What the hell are you doing here?
In the men's game it is not uncommon for the top players to
hold membership on a couple of tours and float from continent to continent, but that kind of cross-pollination is rare
among women. A handful of Americans play full-time in Europe, but for the Italian Open I was one of only two in the
field. (Beth Allen, a California girl coming off four tough years

on the LPGA Tour, was the other.) I got a little friendly trash-talking from my Solheim Cup opponents, but in general all the players were very welcoming. They appreciated that I did a lot of media and promotion throughout the week, helping to publicize a tournament that was nearly canceled due to shaky corporate sponsorship.

Throughout my stay in Milan I felt like an anthropologist observing the differences between the LET and the LPGA. One thing that was immediately noticeable was the shorter workdays among the European players. In the afternoons the driving range and practice putting greens were like ghost towns. It was also interesting to discover the tribal aspect of the tour. In the player dining room all the Swedes were at one table, all the Spaniards at another, all the French girls were sitting together, and so on. Naturally the players spoke in their native tongues. Seeing these cliques provided a little more context to the way the Koreans band together on the LPGA.

The trappings of the Italian Open were similar to an event in America—there were gallery ropes, scoreboards, marshals, the works. The soundtrack was different, though, due to the incessant ringing of cell phones. In the U.S. the tournaments do a good job of discouraging cell phone use and policing the galleries, but everywhere else in the world the fans use them incessantly and the marshals are oblivious or apathetic or both. The crowds were surprisingly large throughout the week—it surely didn't hurt that admission was free—and it was a pretty flashy, well-dressed crowd. It seemed as if they spent more time checking out each other than the golfers. That's cool: We don't care why people show up, as long as they do. Le Rovedine Milano was a good course, though a bit quirky. There was a lot of movement to the holes, sometimes in inconvenient places, forcing numerous layups off the tee.

For the first round I was in one of the featured pairings alongside two Solheim Cuppers: Becky Brewerton, one of the top guns on the LET, and Diana Luna, the goddess of Italian golf. I was definitely a little nervous knowing I was repping the LPGA and that players on both sides of the Atlantic were going to be paying attention to how I fared.

Unfortunately we drew a nine o'clock tee time for the first round. Since arriving in Italy I had been staying up late and sleeping in; rising with the sun for the first round left me feeling lethargic. I sleepwalked through the first ten holes in one over par. Early in the back nine a belated surge of energy kicked in, but I could never quite channel it effectively, as I was feeling restless and trying too hard to make things happen. The result was a nutty finish to my round: birdie, bogey, par, double bogey, eagle, bogey, par, birdie. It all added up to a very frustrating one-over-par 73, leaving me in thirty-second place, six strokes off the lead.

Afterward I raced to the Rodeo Drive of Milan, Via Montenapoleone, to do some shopping before the stores closed. At Versace I nabbed some very sexy thigh-high boots. They were expensive, but nice boots always are. The real killer was the trip to Gucci, where I was unable to resist an oversize blue-and-black python bag. It cost so much I can't even say the amount out loud. Suddenly a good final two rounds became imperative, just to help cover the damage of the shopping spree.

*　　*　　*　　*

The front nine at Le Rovedine has lots of water in play and my approach was a bit too conservative during the second round, leaving me one over par for the first seven holes. On the tee box of the eighth hole—a long, tough par-4—my caddie wandered over and said, "Can I ask a favor?" This was Andy Dearden, who had guided me to such a good finish at the Women's British Open a few months earlier. He had agreed to tote for me until the end of the season, and we enjoyed our usual good chemistry in Italy.

"Sure, whatever," I said.

"You think it would be possible for us to play some fucking golf?"

I was miffed by his cheekiness, and while taking the club back for my tee shot I muttered, "Yeah, like I'm really trying to play like shit right now."

I generally don't like to be challenged by an uppity caddie— my dad included—but this time it worked. I smoked that drive 295 yards down the middle and followed with a wedge to eight feet. When the birdie putt fell in the hole, my caddie shot me a smarmy look and I yelled at him, "Shut up, Andy!"

That set the stage for a spectacular back nine. On the par-5 twelfth hole I pounded a tee shot and then from 230 yards out hit an absolutely pure 3-wood that nestled within nine feet of the hole. Andy offered only one word of analysis: "Dogshit." He didn't mean it. I made the putt for eagle.

At the par-5 fifteenth I got up and down for a birdie. A bogey at sixteen was negated by a great tee shot on the par-3 seventeenth, leading to another birdie. On the par-5 eighteenth I lost my tee shot a little left but from the rough ripped a hybrid to ten feet for another eagle opportunity. As I was eyeing the putt, my mind wandered a bit. I knew everyone associated with the tournament was waiting for me to show them something special. I said to myself, *Well, here's the chance to show 'em.* I nailed the eagle putt—my third in two days—putting an exclamation point on a back-nine 31. My 67 shot me to seventh place, and I have to say it was pretty cool to see a little red, white, and blue on the leaderboard.

That night I went out with Andy and a dozen of his mates. As usual, I was the only girl. We had a great time, talking and laughing and enjoying the fantastic food and wine. Still, I felt a little heavyhearted because my grand Italian adventure was nearing its end.

Starting the final round five strokes off the lead—which was shared by LET legend Laura Davies, of England, and Norway's Marianne Skarpnord—I was determined to get off to a fast start. An eighteen-footer for birdie on the first hole led to my first fist pump of the day. Little did I know it would be my last. After the first hole my putter went cold. That's been a recurring theme this year when I've been in contention to win: The Dinah, Women's British, Portland . . . during all these final rounds it was an inability to convert on the greens that held me back. I wish I could pinpoint the cause beyond the fact that making putts under pressure is the hardest part of competitive golf. (Tiger Woods is the exception that proves the rule.) Swinging the club is an aggressive, dynamic motion, so it's easier to hit shots when you're nervous. Putting is so delicate, and any tension in your arms or wrists or hands can be fatal. When I won tournaments earlier in my career I was nervous coming down the stretch, of course, but my mind-set was to just keep making birdies and not worry about anything else. Now I want to win so badly that it gets harder and harder to block out how much is riding on each putt, which only makes it that much more difficult to sink them.

On the ninth hole I three-putted from twelve feet, pushing me one over par for the round. Winning was no longer a realistic possibility, but I didn't come all the way to Milan to dog it. I regrouped and played a very spirited back nine, making no bogeys and birdying the twelfth and fifteenth holes. Facing an eight-footer for birdie on the final hole, I had an inkling it had to drop for me to finish in the top ten, what would have been a nice little accomplishment. I missed the putt, naturally, shooting a 71 that left me in eleventh place. When I found out my winnings, it really hit home how small the purses are on the LET. My very solid week of golf was worth 3,640 euros, about $5,000. That's roughly last-place money on the LPGA. Skarpnord took home a mere 30,000 euros for her victory. (Winners' checks on the LPGA are never less than $165,000 and usually more like $225,000 and up.) The Italian Open's 200,000 euro total purse was among the smallest on tour, but not that out of line; most are 300,000 euros or less. Playing the LET full-time would definitely curtail my Gucci habit.

The girls on the LET have a reputation for partying hard, so I was bummed to find out that all the players I had become friendly with were flying out following the final round. For my last night in Italy I sure as hell wasn't going to sit around my hotel room, so I hooked up with five friends of a Swedish caddie I had gotten to know a little during the week. It was a bit random, but I was thrilled when I made the acquaintance of my new crew—they were all from Sweden and all very easy on the eyes. I had been dreaming of one last glorious plate of pasta but they insisted on going to Nobu, where they'd snagged a reservation five weeks earlier. So here I was in Milan eating sushi with a bunch of Swedes. Only in Europe.

Afterward we made it past the velvet rope at Armani Privé, a very swank and exclusive nightclub. It was like a Giorgio Armani ad come to life: All the guys were gorgeous but a little scruffy and dangerous looking, and the women were smoking hot and scantily clad. I have to say, though, I was rolling with the best-looking guy in the whole place. Robin was a total Viking, six-foot something, with dreamy blue eyes and sandy blond hair. I had seen Michelangelo's *David* a few days earlier and, trust me, Robin has the better body. We had flirted all through dinner and at the club we had a great time together on the dance floor. I don't really have any dance moves, so I just shook my ass and bumped and grinded all over Robin, who didn't seem to mind.

The next day I bid *arrivederci* to Italy. On the long plane ride home I made a couple of resolutions. One was to marry a Nordic god and raise our trilingual babies in a beautiful villa in Italy. More immediately, I resolved to play more LET events, beginning with the Dubai Ladies Masters in mid-December. This will come a couple of weeks after the LPGA season has ended, and I'm treating it as something of a tourist trip. I've always been intrigued by the Middle East in general and Dubai in particular. Of course I'll try to play some good golf in the midst of all the sightseeing, but no matter what it will be a fun way to end a long year.

During my time in Milan I learned that my big, fat check from the Women's British Open counts toward the LET money list in 2010, so I will have enough exempt status to get into most tournaments. The tour visits so many exotic locations, including three places I'm especially anxious to explore: Turkey, Morocco, and Spain. I'm hoping to play all three tournaments in 2010, schedule permitting. Golf can take you to some amazing places if you're adventuresome enough.

After all the excitement in Milan I wasn't ready to head back to ho-hum Orlando, so I returned to New York City and enjoyed four more days there, again staying at Cristie Kerr's pad. It was great to get to know her on a deeper level. I have always admired Cristie's accomplishments as a golfer, but it turns out there is so much more to her than just a bunch of trophies. She has carved out a nice life for herself as a glam girl-about-town with a very cool husband and myriad charitable pursuits. It's inspiring to see a fellow player with such balance in her life.

I returned to O-town on October 23 for just long enough to get organized for my trip to the Hana Bank–KOLON Championship (HBKC), to be played in Incheon, South Korea. This was the beginning of the final leg of the LPGA season, a mad dash of four tournaments in four weeks in four countries (Korea, Japan, Mexico, the U.S.). There was a lot left to sort out for myself and the tour as a whole. The day before the HBKC tourney began, the LPGA trumpeted the hiring of Mike Whan as our new commissioner. He has a diverse business background, having been a top executive at TaylorMade but also helping to build a couple of sporting-goods companies. Mike has expertise in marketing, which should serve the tour well. He is extremely personable and passionate about golf and he will bring the right energy and temperament to the job. All of us player directors were impressed with him throughout the interview process, and I was honored to have played a small part in helping the LPGA take this big step in moving forward.

Between the ropes, the tour needed the final month to bring some clarity to the season. This was the first year of the post-Annika epoch, and the LPGA had spent 2009 searching for a new identity in the absence of a dominant player to define the season. All four major championships were won by first-time major champions, but none of the victors was able to build on her breakthrough. Lorena Ochoa remained entrenched atop the world ranking, but it had been a pretty rocky year for my old friend. She won two of her first six starts but then went into a five-month swoon (by her incomparable standards), not only failing to win but finishing better than tenth only once. Lorena was candid that she had been distracted by planning her upcoming wedding and adjusting not only to life with a new fiancé but also his three young children from a previous marriage. While Lorena was searching for her old form, the vacuum was filled by Jiyai Shin, a twenty-one-year-old rookie from Korea who won twice in the middle of the year and piled up four other top-ten finishes. Only five foot one, Jiyai is not as explosive as Lorena, but she has no weaknesses in her game. I've been paired with her a handful of times and she just seems to be moseying along—and then you look at her score and it's like, Damn, is she really seven under? Jiyai tries hard but her English is only so-so, so American fans have not yet discovered that she's a pretty fun character. She has a budding singing career and one of her ballads landed on the Korean pop charts. Following the third round of the Samsung World Championship, Jiyai went paragliding above the La Jolla coastline, even though she was leading the tournament.

Lorena may be a sweetheart and a humanitarian, but when it comes to golf she is ferociously competitive. She was never going to relinquish her crown without a brawl, and to no one's surprise she began playing some inspired golf late in the season. She was the runner-up at the CVS/pharmacy LPGA Challenge in Danville and then blew away the field in Alabama, her third win of the year, matching Jiyai's total. The LPGA's Player of the Year race uses a weighted formula that awards 30 points for a victory, 12 points to second place, 9 for third, 7 for fourth, 6 for fifth, et cetera. (Points are doubled for major championships.) Heading into Korea, Jiyai was leading with 136 points while Lorena had 131. A handful of other players still had a chance to steal the award with a rousing finish, notably Cristie Kerr (118), Ai Miyazato of Japan (111), and Suzann Pettersen of Norway (110). I was in twenty-seventh place, with 31 points. Sigh.

My goal for the final month of the season was the same as it had been all year: to win a tournament. But the HBKC was not just another event for me, because of my complicated history there. All the bad mojo started years ago when *Redbook* asked me to name an athlete whom I thought was hot. I picked Apolo Ohno. I mean, c'mon, that skating suit was skintight. You could see *everything*. The magazine came out not long after the 2002 Olympics, at which there was that big controversy when Ohno won a gold medal when his Korean rival was disqualified. One thing about Koreans, we can hold a grudge. I guess because I said something nice about Apolo, it was portrayed in the

Korean media as if I was slighting the entire country. A lot of negative things were written about me before I had ever played a tournament in Korea, and during my first HBKC, in 2003, the press was pretty hostile. It's only gotten worse since, because, as you may have noticed, I'm not one to bite my tongue.

It's worth pointing out that I'm not the only player who feels picked on. All the other Korean-Americans do, too. The press over there loves to write negative things about all of us *gyopos*, as if we chose for our parents to procreate beyond the mystical borders of Korea. Many players have stopped talking to the Korean press altogether. By 2008 I was so fed up I decided to try a new tactic: I would kill 'em with kindness, answering every reporter's question with my biggest, fakest smile. Even that wasn't enough—following that tournament one of the big national newspapers ran a really unfair, inaccurate story. It had its roots in an interview that was conducted on the eve of the final round of the tournament. At the time I was tied for fourth place, only two strokes off the lead. A Korean newspaperman who speaks perfect English asked me, "What would it mean for you to win in this country?"

Luckily, an LPGA official was on hand to tape-record my answer for posterity. This was my verbatim answer, as it was transcribed and posted on lpga.com: "Well, I think it would be kind of a vindication. I understand that I am a controversial person in this country, to say the least, but everyone is entitled to their own opinion. It would be a bit of a vindication for me if I were to come out and win. It would be huge. It's been a long time since I've won. It's been three years just about, and to come back and win, here especially, would be very, very special."

During the tournament coverage my remarks were accurately translated by the Korean media. But a month later *JoongAng Ilbo* ran a story about me in which *vindication* was translated into a word that has an entirely different meaning. It's like *vendetta*, but much stronger. The way the article was written, it basically sounded like I was threatening to cause bodily harm to the Korean public. This wasn't an innocent mistake, something lost in translation. I was so pissed off when the story came out, and so was my dad. Working with lawyers in Korea, we launched a libel lawsuit against the newspaper. This became a little awkward when, in February 2009, the LPGA triumphantly announced a new big-money TV deal that, beginning in 2010, would make the J Golf network the home of the LPGA in Korea. (J Golf also agreed to be the title sponsor for the 2009 Phoenix tour stop and a new tournament in Southern California debuting in 2010.) The problem is that J Golf and *JoongAng Ilbo* are part of the same corporate family, the mighty mass-communications empire of the JoongAng Media Network. Then-commissioner Carolyn Bivens was supportive when I explained the circumstances of the lawsuit, and in my mind the new deal with J Golf only made my little crusade that much more important. The lawsuit would be setting some ground rules heading into the new TV contract, educating the press over there that it's not okay to wantonly smear the LPGA's Korean-Americans.

The libel suit had been gestating all year, and we were still awaiting a resolution as I left for Korea. That didn't make a difference to me—heading over there, my attitude was, I'm not taking shit from anyone anymore.

*   *   *   *

The HBKC is one of the overseas tournaments that pays for the players' airfare and hotel expenses. To cut costs this year, it was ordained that we could not wing in prior to the tournament week, so I didn't get to Incheon until the evening of Monday, October 26. That's a really late arrival—traveling to Asia, I usually like to be settled in at least six days before the first round to allow my body to acclimate to the time (and date) change. I was low-energy throughout the practice rounds, though my play was surprisingly crisp.

Despite my feuding with the media, it's always fun to play in Korea. I enjoy getting to see my extended family and love the energy the fans bring to the tournament. Koreans are unbelievably passionate about golf. They go crazy for any halfway decent shot, even during the practice rounds. They follow the tour quite closely and seem to know everything about the players. Numerous times throughout the week I was recognized away from the golf course, which is always flattering. (This happens only occasionally in the U.S.)

I birdied my very first hole of the tournament, usually a good omen, and went on to shoot a 69 that left me in eleventh place, just three strokes off the lead. Afterward a handful of Korean reporters wanted to talk to me about my round but I blew them off, which I have to admit felt kinda good. Anyway, there wasn't time for chitchat because I had to limp to the on-site physical therapist for some work on my right leg. Every part of my game had been solid during the first round—it was walking the course that gave me problems. Incheon is a big city on the northwest coast about twenty-five miles outside of Seoul; it's as flat as Florida, but the architects of the Sky 72 Golf Club must have moved tons of dirt, because the course has a lot of undulation and some pretty extreme elevation changes.

Walking down the hills was excruciating because earlier in the week I had tweaked my right knee putting in too many miles on the treadmill. Blame it on la dolce vita. Before I left for Italy I had lost thirty-seven pounds in the preceding six months, putting me tantalizingly close to my goal of forty. But I didn't make much time to exercise in Italy, indulging instead on caprese salads, red wine, gelato, and plenty of other mouthwatering treats. I had definitely gained a few pounds over there, so as I was leaving for the HBKC I resolved to run 150 miles before I left for Dubai, which gave me exactly thirty-eight days. (This is typical of my penchant for overdoing it.) During my first few days in Korea I pushed it a little too hard and my right kneecap became swollen and disjointed. On the eve of the first round I had the knee taped up, but that offered only a little relief.

Arriving on the range prior to the second round, my knee and surrounding muscles were a little tight, and temperatures in the forties certainly didn't help. But a bum knee quickly became the least of my worries. When it started pouring rain, Andy discovered that there was no umbrella in my golf bag and, after he pawed through all the pockets, no head cover, either. (This fits over the top of the bag and zips closed to keep the clubs cozy and dry.) Just before I left for Korea a spiffy new bag had arrived from my friends at Keri Golf and my mom volunteered to transfer all my clubs and gear. Apparently she had missed a few things. My dad was hanging out on the range and was able to scrounge up an umbrella, but there was nary a head cover to be found; Andy grabbed about twenty towels and we headed to the first tee. Caddies are obsessive about keeping their players' grips dry in the rain, and I could tell Andy was stressed out about the situation, which made me stressed out, too. Throughout the round he did a phenomenal job tending to my sticks, but while he toweled them dry I had to hold the umbrella. It was a constant juggling act, complicated by a strong wind that almost turned me into Mary Poppins a couple times. From start to finish, it was a frazzling round in brutal conditions. I fought hard and was even par through fourteen holes but three-putted the fifteenth and sixteenth holes to finish with a 74. At the end of the round I was absolutely exhausted, mentally and physically. The good news was that because of the difficult scoring conditions, I only dropped to seventeenth place and was still within four strokes of the lead.

When I arrived at the golf course the next morning for the final round, Andy could tell right away something was wrong. I felt strangely hollow. Here I was playing in Korea with a chance to win—it should have been one of the most exciting rounds of the year, but my heart wasn't in it. It was like everything finally caught up with me: the jet lag, my throbbing knee, the anxiety of facing the Korean media, the fatigue from playing in the rain, all of it coming at the end of a long, emotional year. This downer mood followed me to the course. I bogeyed the second and fourth holes and was overcome with an overpowering sadness. Andy tried to give me a few pep talks, but I couldn't snap out of it. Even a birdie on the seventh hole did nothing to lighten my mood. I sleepwalked through double bogeys on thirteen and sixteen and when the round finally, mercifully ended, I had shot 80, easily my worst round of the season.

My dad is always my toughest critic, but he could sense

something was amiss and immediately after the round he wrapped me in a big hug and just kept whispering, "It's okay, it's okay." My play was so shameful I wanted to avoid all the aunts and cousins and family friends who had gathered in the clubhouse. But someone spotted me and I got roped in. They all tried to pretend like everything was okay, and I did a pretty good job of faking it until my aunt offered me a beautifully wrapped present. I don't know why, but something inside of me snapped and I cried and cried and cried. All the family gathered around me in one big, concerned group hug, but there was nothing they could do to stop the tears. I had let them down, and myself, too.

That night I was still pretty shattered but it was time to move on, at least geographically, as the Mizuno Classic was beckoning. I flew into Nagoya, Japan, and then along with a couple dozen other players took a two-and-a-half-hour bus ride southeast to Shima, in the Mie Prefecture. I needed some time off from golf, so my first day in Japan was spent sleeping in, reading, relaxing, and exploring a zany amusement park with Meaghan Francella and Stacy Lewis.

Tuesday I began trying to rebuild my confidence. This process always starts at the range, with one good shot, then another, and another. I hit hundreds of balls, just trying to groove the feeling of solid contact. I kept telling myself that my awful final round in Korea was nothing more than a fluky confluence of events. But posting a number that big always leaves some scar tissue. By the start of the first round I was feeling better about myself and my game, but I can't say I was feeling good.

For the first round I teed off on the back nine and managed to string together three straight pars. On the par-5 thirteenth hole I hit two excellent shots to reach the green. A so-so lag putt left me four feet for birdie. But I flat-out yipped the putt, missing the hole entirely. I was definitely a little spooked, but I rallied with a sweet twenty-footer for a birdie on number fifteen. The next hole was a par-5 and I should have been thinking about attacking it, but on the tee it was almost as if I was afraid to swing the club. My drive went straight right and settled on a steep hill. I should note here that I hate the turf conditions at Kintetsu Kashikojima Country Club. The ground is brick-hard and the course features this weird Japanese grass with blades that are huge and coarse and unpredictable. I had a gnarly lie for my second shot at sixteen so I slashed at it with a 5-iron, just hoping to get back into the fairway. Much to my surprise, the ball shot out of there like a rocket and rolled all the way across the fairway, through the rough, and into a hazard I didn't even know existed. After some further misadventures I had to make a twenty-footer to save double bogey. Whatever confidence I had built up in the preceding days was now long gone, and I promptly bogeyed the next two holes. A steadier front nine allowed me to salvage a one-over-par 73.

The Japanese fans helped get me out of my funk just a little bit. After the round I signed autographs for about twenty minutes and it was so entertaining. The Japanese galleries aren't as knowledgeable as the Koreans', but they revere us as some kind of visiting goddesses. It's less about appreciating our golfing skill and more like worshipping at the altar of celebrity. When I was signing autographs the people were standing so close, as if they wanted to breathe in my essence. They were begging for a glove, a ball, a tee, any little piece of me they could take home.

In the sixteen hours before my second round I did some heavy-duty soul-searching. The torture of tournament golf can beat down even the best players. It forced Bobby Jones into retirement at age twenty-eight, chased Johnny Miller into the broadcast tower, gave Tom Watson and Bernhard Langer the yips, and left Ian Baker-Finch struggling to break 90. I know I have enough talent to play this game, I just need to believe in myself more, and that was my only goal for the second round. It wound up being a 70, but that relatively ho-hum score doesn't tell the story. I think it was one of the more important rounds of the year. My determination to play better led to a bunch of good shots on the first nine holes. (Again I started on number ten.) I didn't convert any of the birdie chances, and along the way the debilitating sadness I had been feeling on the golf course turned into a more familiar rage. This was a good sign— it showed how much I still cared. On hole number one, a long par-5, I hit two really solid shots just short of the green and then got up and down for birdie. On the third hole I stuck a wedge to two feet, and then on number four hit another lovely approach for my third birdie in the span of four holes. A hard-luck bogey on the ninth hole couldn't spoil what had been a round defined by good play and a rekindled competitive spirit. I definitely have to give Andy some of the credit. He was a steady, positive influence throughout my swoon, and he was instrumental in helping me regain my equilibrium.

That night I felt a little better about the state of my golf game, but overall I wasn't exactly perky. The Mizuno is a funny week because of the setting. Kintetsu Kashikojima Country Club is in the middle of an expansive nature preserve. The players are housed at a hotel next to the club, and for a few days the pastoral tranquillity is very Zen and spiritual. But it's a thirty-dollar cab ride each way to the nearest town, so the players pretty much eat every meal at the hotel and hang out there in the evenings. Ping-Pong grudge matches are fun for a few days, and so is all the endless gossiping, but by the end of the week the hotel feels like a jail, and the players are so sick of each other it's amazing no one gets shanked in the dining room.

Unfortunately, my putter overslept for the final round and I again blew a bunch of birdie chances. I was even par on my round with two holes to go but finished bogey, double bogey for a 75 that dropped me to a woeful sixty-second place.

I had a long flight home to stew about my Asian malaise. My struggles in Japan were really a result of the bad mojo from Korea, where I let myself get overwhelmed. It was a painful learning experience but will serve me well for future trips. I've always wanted to play well in Korea, for a variety of reasons, but I'm now going to treat that tournament like my fifth major. Sooner or later, I will have my vindication.

CHAPTER 13

The End of the Road

Shima, Japan, to Guadalajara, Mexico, is not a well-traveled route. Sophie Gustafson tweeted that it was a mind-boggling (and neck-kinking) forty-six hours from the time she left Kintetsu Kashikojima Country Club until she reached her hotel in Guadalajara, site of the Lorena Ochoa Invitational, the penultimate tournament of the year. I was spared the hassle because I didn't qualify for the extremely limited field, which is reserved for the top thirty-one players on the money list. (I was thirty-sixth at the cutoff, which followed the Navistar LPGA Classic in Alabama.) The field is filled out with five sponsor's exemptions. My agents had lobbied tournament organizers, but ultimately the invitations went to all-time greats Juli Inkster and Laura Davies, crowd favorite Natalie Gulbis, and the Spanish-speaking duo of Sophia Sheridan, from Mexico, and Mariajo Uribe of Colombia. I never talked to Lorena directly about the sponsor's exemption because I didn't want to put her on the spot. The tournament may carry her name but a lot of people are part of the decision making, and I didn't take it personally that the exemptions had gone to other players. Bottom line, I could have qualified on my own and didn't get it done.

Of course I was bummed to miss out on the Lorena lovefest. She grew up on the host venue, Guadalajara Country Club, and the adoration is unlike anything I've ever seen. We were paired together for the third round in 2008 and it was like playing golf with the pope. When Lorena walked anywhere near the rope line, people would literally hold out their babies hoping she would touch them, and a few slipped her rosaries or religious medals. Naturally, Lorena was wearing her heart on her sleeve the whole time. It was an amazing experience to see that up close.

While Lorena's tournament was playing out, I returned home to Orlando. After the downer trip to Asia I obviously needed to right myself, but I wasn't worried about anything technical in my golf game. My goal was simply to have fun on the course again. Yes, golf is my job, but it's always been a joy and a passion. I needed to rekindle some of that old love of the game.

Luckily, one of my close friends on tour, Jeehae Lee, proposed a road trip to Daytona Beach. Only the top eighty on the final money list secure their playing privileges for the following season; Jeehae wasn't going to make enough in her rookie year and was thus headed back to the dreaded Qualifying tournament (aka "Q School") in Daytona. She wanted to scout the course at which she would be playing for her livelihood. Jane Park came, too, and we had a blast. On the golf course we cranked hip-hop through my iPhone and were laughing and dirty dancing and talking trash about our various money games. It was exactly what I needed.

It also felt good to help Jeehae with her preparations. The LPGA has a mentoring program for its rookies and at the start of the year I had been designated her "big sister," which was kind of funny given that Jeehae is actually a year older than I am and about four inches taller. She had played golf at the tony Phillips Academy in Andover, Massachusetts, but gave up playing competitively after a year at Yale, choosing instead to focus on her economics degree. After college she got the itch to play again and turned pro. Yeah, Jeehae is an Ivy Leaguer, and she speaks four languages (French, Korean, Mandarin Chinese, and perfect English), and she also happens to be drop-dead gorgeous. She is a tremendous asset for the tour, and will be even more so when she achieves her considerable potential as a player. The fact that she was stressing about keeping her job gave me a little dose of perspective. It hadn't been the year I wanted, but at thirty-seventh on the money list I was guaranteed a spot on tour in 2010, which wasn't true for many other very talented golfers.

After four days at home I headed to Houston on Saturday, November 14, to get settled in for the season-ending Tour Championship. The next day I was glued to the tube watching the final round of the Lorena Ochoa Invitational. It was a very momentous week for the tour. At the start of the tournament, the big story was the ongoing Player of the Year race. Jiyai Shin had stretched her lead over Lorena by finishing sixth in Korea. Jiyai was propelled by the raucous following of her countrymen, who turned out en masse for the chance to witness history. For all the success the Koreans have had on the LPGA,

none of them have ever been Player of the Year. Jiyai had already clinched Rookie of the Year honors—the fifth Korean to
take the award since Se Ri Pak's breakthrough in 1998—but if
she could double-dip as POY she would become only the second player to earn both awards in the same year, matching
Nancy Lopez's iconic feat from 1978. Lorena added to the intrigue with a spectacular performance the next week in Japan,
making only one bogey in fifty-four holes and shooting the
tournament's low round on Sunday, a 64 that propelled her to
a tie for second place. That cut Jiyai's lead in the POY points
race to 147–143, setting up a showdown in Guadalajara. Even
though the home crowd was openly (but politely) rooting
against her, Jiyai played well enough to finish tied for third,
what I consider to be one of the ballsiest performances of the
year. Lorena nearly kept pace, finishing sixth and thus extend-
ing the drama to the Tour Championship. It would be the first
time since 1994 that the Player of the Year race came down to
the final tournament. But by Sunday in Guadalajara no one was
talking POY anymore because Michelle Wie shot a rock-solid
final-round 69 to win her first pro tournament, at long last.

I got to see her game firsthand at the Solheim Cup and there
was never any doubt Michelle was going to win soon. And she
did it in high style at the Ochoa Invitational, fighting off a bevy
of world-class players and then, on the seventy-second hole,
hitting the shot of a lifetime to clinch the win: a thirty-yard
bunker shot that spun to a stop inches from the hole. The victory was a testament to the maturation of Michelle's game, and
the celebration was evidence of how she had become such a big
part of the culture of the tour this year: Solheim teammates
Brittany Lincicome and Morgan Pressel joyously showered her

with beer on the final green. That night I sent a text to Michelle with a simple message: "Welcome to the winners' club." I was so happy for her on a personal level, and every LPGA player realized what an important milestone it was for the tour. No one in women's golf moves the needle like Michelle, which was evident when *USA Today* put her victory on 1A. She will bring a tremendous amount of attention to the tour in 2010 and beyond, and that's going to help all of us.

The timing of Michelle's victory was ironic because two days later, during a players' meeting at the season-ending Tour Championship, LPGA officials unveiled the 2010 schedule, which featured twenty-four tournaments. (A twenty-fifth was later added.) Given how dire things looked during the summer, it felt like a victory that we were down only three events from the 2009 slate. Our new commissioner, Mike Whan, stood at the front door before the meeting to shake hands with all of the players, the first time most were meeting him. With his new energy and Michelle's star power and the incredible international popularity of the players (highlighted by Lorena and Jiyai), it feels as if the LPGA is on the verge of some big things heading into a new TV contract and, hopefully, a better economy.

Still, all the uncertainty surrounding the tour had created a lot of anxiety among the players and, in the end, I was a victim of the blowback. During the same player meeting that the schedule was unveiled, a vote was taken among the membership to fill out two player-director spots on the LPGA's board. I had to run for reelection, and Kim Hall and Katie Futcher nominated themselves. Both are very bright, well-spoken girls— Kim holds a degree from Stanford, while Katie got hers at Penn

State—and prior to the vote they gave excellent speeches to their fellow players. During my spiel I expressed what an honor it was to have served and emphasized my passion for the tour and my desire to continue to help guide it. But when the votes were tallied, I had been booted off the board.

I'm not gonna lie, it stung. I don't take rejection well. Afterward, so many players gave me hugs and said they appreciated all of my hard work. Not to accuse anyone of being fake, but all I could think was, *Really? Because if all of you had voted for me, I would have been reelected easily.* Afterward a couple of wise veterans supplied an interesting analysis. They pointed out that the Tour Championship, with 120 players in the field, was for many of the girls their first playing opportunity in a month and a half, due to the limited fields in Asia and Mexico. And that neither Kim nor Katie had ever finished in the top seventy of the money list, whereas I'd never been out of the top fifty. So maybe it was the LPGA's version of class warfare that cost me my spot on the board. Hearing that helped my ego, but just barely.

I went out that night with Michelle Wie and a few other players. We were theoretically celebrating Michelle's victory, but it also gave me a nice opportunity to drown my sorrows with a couple of Tanqueray and tonics.

For the first round of the Tour Championship I landed in the tournament's marquee pairing alongside Michelle and Cristie Kerr. Texans love their golf, and our gallery was huge. I was already putting a lot of pressure on myself to end the year on a high note. Finishing, say, a solid fifteenth didn't really interest me. That wouldn't change the contours of my season. But having a chance to win could definitely improve how I felt about what had been an up-and-down year.

Unfortunately, we didn't have the luck of the draw, getting an afternoon tee time in high winds after what had been a calm, easy morning. On the par-3 fourth hole I hit a pretty decent tee shot but it was blown way off line by the gales, leading to a bogey. The eighth hole was a killer. I missed the green, hit a so-so chip, and then three-putted from twenty feet for a brutal double bogey.

Heading to the back nine I should have focused on just playing solid shots and not blowing myself out of the tournament. Unfortunately, I was impatient and greedy, trying to force the action. On the par-5 twelfth hole I pulled my drive but it took a lucky hop and barely stayed out of a water hazard that runs the length of the hole. It was a great break and put me in good position for a birdie. I wanted an eagle. Even though the wind was howling from right to left toward the hazard, and even though I had a hook lie, I went for the green from 210 yards out. The shot started a touch left of where I was aiming and the wind did the rest, blowing my ball into the hazard. Bogey. It was a stupid shot and I was still pretty unsettled playing the next hole. Protecting against the water that guarded the left side of the thirteenth green, I fanned my approach shot way right, and after a fluffed chip I made double bogey. My round—and any hope of salvation—had been ruined.

My 79 looked even worse next to Michelle's 72. She had sprained her ankle at the Solheim Cup and kept aggravating the injury in the ensuing months. Her limp had gotten progressively worse in Guadalajara, and after the victory Michelle would've loved to withdraw from the Tour Championship. But she knew that would've been a monumental buzzkill, and she felt an obligation to support the tournament and the tour. To take pressure off the ankle she manufactured a Gary Player–like follow-through in which she chased after the shot instead of keeping her left side planted. Still, the ankle buckled on her tee shot on the par-3 seventeenth hole and her ball came up twenty yards short, in a lake. On her drive on number eighteen Michelle's ankle collapsed again. By that point we were both feeling so sorry for ourselves we shared a hug walking down the eighteenth fairway that lasted about one hundred yards. Michelle had shown so much heart making it through the round, but that evening she withdrew from the tournament, getting out of town just in time.

A biblical storm arrived on Friday morning and made a royal mess of the next three days. I got up at five A.M. for my eight-twenty second-round tee time and arrived at the course just in time for play to be suspended. After hours of sitting around, the LPGA decided to send us out in a driving rain. Because of the lack of daylight in mid-November, there was no way the afternoon times would tee off, so only the morning wave would have to play in the miserable conditions. I thought it was a very unfair decision, and this feeling of persecution helped me focus better on the course. I played a solid front nine, making one birdie and one bogey for an even-par 36 despite the nasty weather. As Cristie Kerr and I made the turn, play was suspended due to darkness.

A second-round restart was called for seven A.M. on Saturday. I was pretty dubious that would happen, having fallen asleep and then awakened to the sound of falling raindrops. Still, I had to go through the motions, so I was up at four A.M. and at the course by five thirty. It was still pouring rain but no postponement had been announced, so all the players warmed up in the predawn blackness under floodlights. An hour later I was soaked to the bone. At this point the sun had peeked through and LPGA officials quickly decided that the course was—surprise!—still unplayable; play was suspended yet again. All the players trudged to the clubhouse and you've never heard so much bitching and moaning in your life! Every two hours the LPGA reassessed the conditions, declared them unplayable, and told us to hang loose until the next announcement. I ate breakfast four times, played poker, watched music videos on a laptop, and took a power nap on a clubhouse couch. Finally, around one P.M., tour officials decided what the players had known all along: The day was a washout. The Tour Championship was shortened to fifty-four holes with a Monday finish. Hopefully.

To kill time that afternoon, Jeehae Lee and Jane Park and I went shopping. We wound up at a dress shop. Now, this is Texas, so everything is a little gaudy anyway, but this place was totally over the top and we were not surprised to be told that it's a favorite of big-haired young women on the beauty-pageant circuit. Jane and Jeehae and I were giggling hysterically as we tried on the dresses. They were so bad they were good, and I actually bought one, a bejeweled multilayer blue-green silk thingy that Barbie would love.

The next morning I was up before sunrise for a third straight day. Just as I pulled into the golf course parking lot, a text message informed me that play was suspended until at least noon. It was like *Groundhog Day* without the laughs. In the locker room I spied a newspaper with the headline WEATHER WOES FOR CURSED LPGA. That pretty much summed it up. Eventually that afternoon I got to complete my second round. Thanks to my little rally on the front nine *forty-eight hours* earlier, there was still a chance to make the cut if I went really low, but after all the mind-numbing delays I wasn't feeling much dramatic tension. When I bogeyed the first hole of the day, it was clear the golf gods did not want me to make the cut. I played the next eight holes in two under, but it wasn't enough. On the final hole I tapped in for a par to tidy up a 71. Just like that, my season was over.

From a statistical perspective, 2009 has to be considered my worst season since I was a clueless rookie six years earlier. I finished thirty-eighth on the money list ($344,055), my worst showing since '03. That was the only year I've ever had more missed cuts than my five in '09. My scoring average (72.29, forty-ninth on tour), greens in regulation (66.9 percent, fifty-seventh), and driving accuracy (69.4 percent, eighty-second) stats were all worse than my career averages.

As erratic as my play was, I still enjoyed three of the best weeks of my career. Going 3–1 at the Solheim Cup was the highlight of the year, and it means everything to me to have proven myself again in that event. With any luck I'll compete in another six or seven Solheims, and hopefully they will go a long way toward defining me as a player.

The other really significant development of '09 was that I was right there on Sunday with a chance to win two different major championships. Lorena Ochoa can't say that, or Jiyai Shin, or Michelle Wie, or a bunch of other big names. Most players have to lose a couple of majors before they win their first one. My near misses at the Kraft Nabisco Championship and the Women's British Open prove to me that I can take my game to a much higher level, if only I can learn to summon that focus and confidence on a more regular basis. Those tournaments were phenomenal learning experiences, and the lessons will be applied at future major championships. Before this year I thought I was good enough to win a major, but I wasn't completely sure. Now I'm certain I can do it.

A lot of other things fell into place for me this year. After endless tinkering, I finally discovered the right mix of equipment and didn't change a thing after the middle of the season. I'm also thrilled to have found Andy Dearden for a caddie. He's agreed to stay on my bag forever (or at least until one of us changes our mind). He is the perfect personality for me, and I think we're going to continue to build on the success we had at the British and Italian Opens. I'm such a control freak, I've never let any of my caddies help me enough. During the pro-am at the Tour Championship I was a little low on energy, so I told Andy I was going to shut off my brain and let him do all the thinking. He would say, "It's one hundred and fifty-eight yards but a little uphill with a hurting wind, so I like a low, cut six-iron starting five yards left of the flag that will funnel off the slope to a back flag." Then I would step up and hit the exact shot he wanted. He also read my putts beautifully. It was a fun way to play and the partnership helped keep both of us engaged. I will look forward to letting go a little bit more in the future and giving Andy a chance to improve my course management.

Setting aside all the golf stuff, 2009 was all about my personal metamorphosis. The physical change is the most obvious; with some heroic restraint over the holidays, I finally dropped my fortieth pound and I am pretty damn proud of myself for achieving such a weighty goal. I've resolved to improve my fitness in a more dynamic way over the off-season, lifting weights with a trainer to increase my strength and flexibility. I've always stayed away from weights out of fear of becoming too bulky, but I finally decided that's ridiculous—I'm a professional athlete, and my body needs to be the most efficient machine possible. It's okay to have a few muscles. I just need to find a guy who's not intimidated by powerful femininity.

Actually, finding a guy is not that high on my to-do list. One very important thing I learned this year is that I can be happy on my own. I went from being a semi-subservient Korean daughter who traveled with her parents straight into my first long-term relationship, during which my boyfriend was almost always on the road with me. So 2009 was really the first time I was living life by myself, and I finally got to know who I am. Yes, I led the LPGA in tears shed, but from all the hard times I developed a newfound strength. It was empowering to discover I can make it just fine without having a boyfriend or parent around as an emotional crutch. Even though I strengthened numerous friendships and made some very important new ones, I learned to love my alone time, during which I read a bunch of mind-expanding books on my Kindle. I also spent a couple thousand dollars on iTunes, much of it going toward downloading my favorite TV shows. There were many nights on the road when I was utterly content to soak in the bath and watch *South Park* or *Lie to Me* or *Futurama* or *Burn Notice* or *Law & Order SVU* or a dozen other shows on my laptop.

So many things this year brought me to where I am now: the breakup with Mark, growing closer with my parents, the nasty

bout of food poisoning, having the Golf Channel audience listen in on my miked-up humiliation at the LPGA Championship, harmless flirtations with various boys, my torn eyeball,
media controversies, and numerous little on-course triumphs
leavened by occasional bouts of crushing self-doubt. It was the
longest, hardest year of my life, on and off the course, but also
the most important. A season can be judged a success or failure
in a lot of different ways, but for me I'll remember 2009 for a
simple reason: It was the year I finally grew up.

Walking off my final green at the Tour Championship I was
numb, just kind of overwhelmed by the harsh finality to the end
of the season. I really didn't know how to feel, and I was still in a
daze while signing my scorecard. But stepping outside of the
scorer's tent I got a little jolt when I was confronted by a noisy
throng of autograph seekers. Those Houston fans are pretty
impressive—they just kept coming back, despite the endless delays and sloppy course conditions. They would be rewarded
during the Monday finish, when the nerve-jangling Player of the
Year race came down to the final hole. Lorena Ochoa made one
last clutch birdie to lock up second place at the Tour Championship and surge past Jiyai Shin in the point totals, 160–159,
nabbing her fourth straight POY award. It was thrilling stuff, and
the crowds went bonkers for Lorena. Golf fans will always gravi-
tate to the biggest stars. Someday I hope to be in that rarefied air,
but if I've learned anything this year it's that I just gotta be me; I
have something to offer even if my game is in a funk. So when
I found myself face-to-face with all those fans at the Tour Championship, I became determined to make a good impression. I

spent the next forty-five minutes signing autographs, and I was my sparkliest and most animated self. I cleaned out my golf bag, signing and giving away all of my balls, gloves, and stray paraphernalia. I took photos with the fans, doled out hugs, and generally had a great time letting all of them know how much I appreciate their support. In the midst of spreading all this good cheer, it really hit home that my own little drama about missing the cut meant nothing to these people. They were just happy for the interaction. That I have the ability to spread this kind of joy is an honor and a responsibility I don't take lightly. Even though golf occasionally beats me up, I know I'm so lucky to be living my dream.

In that mass of fans I had a nice chat with a teenage girl who said her goal is to someday play on the LPGA. Maybe in seven or eight years she will make it to the tour. I know one thing: If she does, I'll be here waiting for her. When the 2010 season begins, I'll still be only twenty-five. Having spent this year figuring out so many things, I'm very bullish about the future. In fact, I feel like I'm just getting started.

A NOTE ON THE AUTHORS

Christina Kim has been one of the LPGA's most popular players since 2003, when she was a nineteen-year-old rookie. A two-time winner on tour, she was also a key member of the victorious U.S. Solheim Cup teams in 2005 and 2009. Born and raised in San Jose, California, she now lives in Orlando.

Alan Shipnuck has been covering professional golf for *Sports Illustrated* since 1994. He is the author of the national bestseller *Bud, Sweat, & Tees: Rich Beem's Walk on the Wild Side of the PGA Tour.* He lives in Salinas, California, with his wife and children.